MODERN NAVAL WARFARE

Eight decades of naval evolution

Welcome to this special publication in which we set out to investigate naval warfare post-World War Two. That global conflict saw naval battles and campaigns larger than any in history, before or since. The technologies that emerged during that war – nuclear weapons and power, guided missiles and jet aircraft – influenced naval weaponry and doctrine into the Cold War. By the late 20th century, digital technology and advances in electronics mated these new weapons to advanced sensors, precision targeting systems, and ever-increasing computing power. The result is naval forces able to project power over wide areas of the oceans and deep inland from the coasts.

The advanced naval capabilities of today are an evolution of not only technology but decades of combat experience in dozens of wars and military operations from 1946 to today. In this publication we will examine many of these conflicts, focusing on those which influenced modern tactical and strategic thought. Most took place in current hotspots and potential crisis points. The current actions and tensions in the waters around the Middle East and Taiwan Strait are only the latest chapters in the naval histories of those regions.

Over the past eight decades, naval engagements have occurred in the warm waters of the Persian Gulf, the Pacific Ocean and Mediterranean Sea down to the cold waters of the South Atlantic. A few were over in hours while others went on for years or decades. One threatened to spark a nuclear war while several were so localised few people have ever heard of them.

Finally, we look at the latest and upcoming naval technologies, the future naval environment and the likely tactics of coming naval warfare. Four of today's expected crisis points are evaluated as to how a naval war might play out. We hope these looks at the future of naval warfare provoke thought about what might be coming for the world's navies. Large naval battles may still be ahead in future conflicts, bigger and more deadly than anything seen in nearly a century. Enjoy this publication!

ABOVE: HMS *Dragon* fires her 4.5in cannon during gunnery practice. UK MoD Crown Copyright

BELOW: Carrier Strike Group 21 (HMS *Queen Elizabeth*) steams with British, American and Dutch escort ships during a worldwide cruise in 2021. UK MoD Crown Copyright

MAIN COVER IMAGE: The USS *Gerald R. Ford* (CVN78) Petty Officer 3rd Class Riley Mc. US Navy

CONTENTS

Modern Naval Warfare

ABOVE: An F35 Lightning of 617 squadron receives the take-off signal aboard HMS *Queen Elizabeth*. UK MoD Crown Copyright

MAIN IMAGE: An international naval force sails in formation during the Rim of the Pacific (RIMPAC) exercise, 2024. US Navy

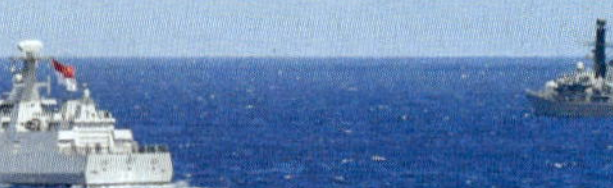

THE FUTURE

ABOVE: A Russian corvette launches a Kalibr cruise missile. Russian MoD

SCENARIOS

ISBN: 978 1 83632 129 3
Editor: Chris Miskimon
Senior editor, specials: Roger Mortimer
Email: roger.mortimer@keypublishing.com
Cover Design: Steve Donovan
Design: SJmagic DESIGN SERVICES, India
Advertising Sales Manager: Sam Clark
Email: sam.clark@keypublishing.com
Tel: 01780 755131
Advertising Production: Becky Antoniades
Email: Rebecca.antoniades@keypublishing.com

SUBSCRIPTION/MAIL ORDER
Key Publishing Ltd, PO Box 300, Stamford, Lincs, PE9 1NA
Tel: 01780 480404
Subscriptions email: subs@keypublishing.com
Mail Order email: orders@keypublishing.com
Website: www.keypublishing.com/shop

PUBLISHING
Group CEO: Adrian Cox
Publisher: Steve O'Hara

Published by
Key Publishing Ltd, PO Box 100, Stamford, Lincs, PE9 1XQ
Tel: 01780 755131
Website: www.keypublishing.com

PRINTING
Precision Colour Printing Ltd, Haldane, Halesfield 1, Telford, Shropshire. TF7 4QQ

DISTRIBUTION
Seymour Distribution Ltd, 2 Poultry Avenue, London, EC1A 9PU
Enquiries Line: 02074 294000.

ABOVE: The Aurora Borealis shines above HMS *Albion* during Exercise Cold Response, 2022. UK MoD, Crown Copyright

MODERN NAVAL WARFARE

Conflict and change since 1945

Change and adaptation are the hallmarks of modern navies and of naval warfare since 1945. World War Two saw enormous fleets operating across the globe, using the latest weapons and equipment. Radar allowed those fleets to find each other, direct their fire and detect incoming flights of aircraft. Those aircraft evolved quickly during the war, becoming much more capable in terms of endurance, speed and payload. Even long-serving weapons received significant improvements; cannon shells received new fuses and torpedoes improved.

Tactical and operational concepts also improved greatly. Those nations possessing aircraft carriers – the United Kingdom, United States and Japan – learned how to group carriers to manoeuvre them to advantage and mass their firepower. By 1943 the Allies learned how to reduce the threat of the submarine through convoys and by forming dedicated antisubmarine hunter-killer groups using a combination of dedicated aircraft and ships designed for the role. Amphibious warfare saw its development rise to a high standard, with the creation of dedicated landing ships and craft, and surface combatants to provide fire support. By 1945 the UK and US possessed advanced capabilities in all these areas.

Added to these techniques and weapons were new inventions just entering service at the war's end. Though in their developmental infancy, they pointed the way to the future. Two in particular would drastically change naval warfare – guided missiles and jet aircraft. Together, they radically increased the striking range and power of naval vessels.

Guided missiles saw their first limited use in action in 1943 by the Germans and continued with the V-1 and V-2 weapons. While of minimal military effectiveness at the time, their employment by the Nazis as terror weapons against civilians did show their potential for further refinement. By 1945 the Allies were experimenting with their own guided missiles and bombs, field testing them in Europe and Southeast Asia.

The Germans introduced jet aircraft to combat as well, though they appeared too late and, in too few numbers, to affect the course of the war. Anglo-American designs arrived too late for combat use, but their initial models entered service soon after the war, enabling more refined designs to fly in the Korean War in 1950. The potential of jet aircraft led to intensive development as the Cold War split the world into East and West. The capabilities of jets improved rapidly in the 1950s and 1960s. Shore based strike aircraft could pose a significant threat to naval vessels and the new carrier planes compelled navies to radically update their existing aircraft carriers and build much larger new ones.

Nuclear weapons also affected naval development postwar. Navies were forced to operate in a more dispersed fashion to avoid losing an entire fleet to one bomb. Likewise, massed amphibious operations were now also risky. Conversely, nuclear powers soon developed nuclear weapons for their navies, most significantly the Sea-Launched Ballistic Missile (SLBM) carried aboard submarines. Difficult to locate and destroy, such submarines added an air of uncertainly to any adversaries war plans.

BELOW: The rapidly changing nature of naval operations compels militaries to find innovative ways to increase firepower. This US Marine Corps HIMARS launcher is firing from the flight deck of an amphibious assault ship. USMC

As navies evolved during the Cold War, these new weapons were employed through improved radars, reconnaissance and surveillance, electronic warfare and communications systems. This included the use of satellites orbiting high overhead. Once the electronics revolution began the digital age, such systems improved by orders of magnitude, much faster than the weapons themselves.

One significant benefit of the digital age is the addition of precision munitions. The ability to land a munition within a few metres of its target drastically reduced the number of missiles or bombs required to destroy it. This meant a ship could stay on station longer before depleting its munition supply. Air strikes can be effective using only one or two aircraft; previously it might have required a squadron or more with extensive support to achieve the same effect. These weapons also reduced, though did not eliminate, noncombatant casualties and collateral damage when responsibly employed.

Technological advances have increased naval capabilities and changed the way information is gathered, organised and used. The basic and essential missions of navies have changed little, however. Most nations operate small navies which are essentially coastal defence forces. They protect local shipping from piracy, act to prevent crime and smuggling, conduct inspections and occasionally engage a neighbour's military during a conflict.

The navies of more powerful nations perform those roles but significantly have the ability to project power beyond their coastal waters. This requires naval forces beyond those needed for pure defence, which requires the nation to have the economic capacity to support a large navy. They patrol international shipping lanes and support their nation's interests abroad. Navies remain an instrument of their nation's political desire and will.

The obvious example of this is the US Navy, which has acted to guarantee overall freedom of navigation on the world's oceans since 1945. This benefits the United States due to its policies of free trade but other nations benefit too as the policy frees them of the expense of the larger navies they might otherwise need. Admittedly, it can also make them dependent on the US for protection of their own interests. While this can be constraining, powerful navies are hideously expensive and working with a large power is often less costly and achieves the desired result.

A good example of naval balance is the Australian Navy. As an island nation distant from many foreign markets, it must simultaneously possess the naval power to protect its coastline and project power abroad to protect shipping and take part in operations with allies when necessary. As an island in close proximity to other island nations, some of which are significantly smaller, it must also be able to carry out support, relief and amphibious operations as needed. Australia's navy possesses a variety of ship types to carry out all these missions. However, Australia cannot build a navy large enough to protect it in »

ABOVE: A British Wildcat helicopter fires flares over the Norwegian frigate *Otto Sverdrup* during an exercise. Flares distract infrared homing weapons by giving them something hotter than the intended target to track. UK MoD Crown Copyright

LEFT: The battleship USS *Missouri* bombards Chongjin, North Korea in October 1950. Though the era of the battleship ended in World War Two, the US Navy kept the four Iowa class ships in and out of service until the 1990s. US Navy

LEFT: China's rapid naval expansion includes large numbers of submarines, both nuclear and conventional. This submarine of the Northern Theatre Command is underway in 2025. Chinese MoD

LEFT MIDDLE: Submarine hunting matches antiship and air defence as vital roles for warships. The Russian corvette *Kalmykiya* fires its RBU-6000 antisubmarine rocket launcher. Russian President's Office

a major war, so it also works with allies such as the UK and US. This willingness to be part of a larger alliance system serves Australian economic needs while bringing the high quality of its military, which 'punches above its weight,' into the service of its alliances.

Since World War Two, that system of alliances, such as NATO and others has served to prevent a major war from occurring. It has not deterred a myriad of smaller wars and conflicts from breaking out. Most of these have involved naval forces to some degree. Only one, the Falklands Crisis, has involved a fleet-sized action well out to sea, and even that centred around the recovery of the islands. Almost all naval operations have occurred along

BELOW: The northern lights shine above HMS *Prince of Wales* during night operations. An effective modern navy must have air cover to project power, and carriers numbers are increasing among the world's navies. UK MoD Crown Copyright

ABOVE: These grainy images show the effect of a Tomahawk cruise missile on an obsolete US destroyer. Tomahawks carry a 1,000lb high explosive warhead. US Navy

coastlines, also called the littoral zones, or over smaller islands or waters adjacent to land features, such as straits.

This is the normal state of affairs. Large wars with battles out at sea are actually the exception; navies spend most of their time fighting close to land, as that is where the populations they wish to defend or impose their will on reside. World War Two was actually an outlier, though one enormous in scope and importance.

What followed, the active naval operations of the Cold War, were also mainly centred on fighting in the littorals, although the East-West nature of the overall conflict meant the world's navies had to be ready to fight a major war at sea again. The Cold War saw much focus on the aircraft carrier as a means of power projection along with the submarine, partly due to their stealth and partly to the development of the ballistic missile submarine. While carriers saw wide use, submarines were markedly less useful for littoral fights, though they proved useful in a deterrent role and in various covert operations.

After the Cold War ended in 1991, the threat of a major war receded, leaving the US and its allies unchallenged for a time. The focus became maritime cooperation and preserving freedom of navigation. The attacks of September 11, 2001, took the focus to supporting operations against terrorism. Meanwhile, as Chinese economic power grew, so did its navy. The Russians, although still nowhere near the size or power of the Soviet Navy, reconstituted to a great degree.

Now, the threat of large-scale naval warfare has returned, though such a war is far from certain. Compared to World War Two, there are far fewer ships, but each surface combatant is a floating fortress of missiles while carriers enable far ranging operations. Many nations which cannot afford supercarriers are instead building smaller models which can operate the F-35B or armed UAS, the next evolution in naval airpower. While naval operations against terror movements and rogue nations will no doubt continue, the chance of a new Pacific War (see page 110) or a new Battle of the Atlantic (see page 108) loom in the imaginations of naval planners.

RIGHT: The USS *Enterprise* sails under the Golden Gate Bridge in San Francisco, California in 1983. The large aircraft carrier has been a foundation of US naval power since World War Two. NARA

RIGHT: Western navies have spent decades learning to operate together under combat conditions and this effort has paid off in recent operations. Here, HMS *Brazen* joins a strike group centred around USS *Midway* in 1984. US Navy

GUIDED MISSILES

A defining weapon of modern naval warfare

One of the defining changes in warships after 1945 was the rise of the guided missile as a primary weapon. Though major surface combatants still carry several types of cannon systems for close range defence, shore bombardment and anti-aircraft use, the missile is now their go-to offensive option. They come in several varieties, each generally tailored for a particular mission, although technological advances are enabling many new designs to be multi-use.

Anti-ship Missiles are designed for specific use against ships, though many designs have a dual use against land targets. Most designs are 'sea-skimmers,' meaning they fly only a few metres above the water to make detection more difficult. They can be carried by ships, large boats, aircraft including helicopters, and submarines. Ashore, they are often carried on vehicles such as large lorries. This provides better survivability than placing them in a fixed launcher installation, as mobile launchers can move and hide to avoid detection and counterfire.

Defending against anti-ship missiles is difficult. A ship's search radar can detect a sea skimming missile at 15-18 miles due to the curvature of the earth. That provides 30-60 seconds of warning if the missile is subsonic. This does not give the crew much time to launch chaff or fire defensive weapons.

Land Attack Missiles (LAM) are optimised for striking targets ashore. This allows naval forces to influence operations ashore at ranges much farther than the range of their cannon. Indeed, several designs have range exceeding 1,000 miles (1,600 km), allowing precision strikes far inland. Like antiship missiles, most

ABOVE: The Arleigh Burke class destroyer USS *Mustin* fires a pair of SM-2 missiles during an exercise. The SM-2 is now the primary surface to air missile for the USN, replacing two earlier designs. US Navy

LEFT: Before the advent of launch cells, many warships used rotating launchers which were reloaded automatically from a magazine below deck. This is a US Mk 11 launcher aboard the destroyer USS *Lawrence* in 1983. US Navy

LAMs fly very low and are often equipped with terrain-following guidance systems containing preprogrammed information about their course.

ABOVE: The Brahmos cruise missile is a joint venture between India and Russia which can also be fired from submarines, aircraft and land-based launchers. Here, the frigate INS *Nilgiri* fires one in 2025. Indian Government

Surface to Air Missiles (SAMs) defend against aerial threats, most commonly aircraft. However, newer designs also function against incoming missiles and Unmanned Aerial Systems (UAS). The initial models were often divided into short, medium and long-range systems, though modern designs tend towards longer ranges. This is growing more important as the missiles carried by aircraft are of increasingly longer range to give them better stand-off capability. It is always better to shoot down an enemy plane before it can launch its ordnance. A few designs, such as the US Standard Missile (SM) series, can also function in the anti-ship role if needed.

Air to Surface Missiles (ASM) are carried by aircraft for anti-ship or land attack use. They are an important part of the firepower of aircraft carriers, particularly as modern long-range ASMs allow the carrier to engage targets farther outside their airwing's combat radius. Similarly, such weapons carried by land-based aircraft extend the range at which attacking naval forces can be engaged, forcing them to fight through a larger engagement zone to reach the protected coastline. Helicopters frequently carry small ASMs which can be particularly effective against patrol craft and small boats. The Royal Navy used such weapons effectively in the Falklands conflict (see page 62) and the US Navy did so in the Persian Gulf during Operation Praying Mantis (see page 72). One subcategory is the anti-radiation missile, designed to home in on the radar emissions of SAMs and radio communications sources.

Air to Air Missiles (AAM): Aircraft have been one of the major threats to naval forces since World War Two, when fighter Combat Air Patrols (CAPs) protected important assets, such as carriers, from enemy strikes. As missile technology progressed after the war, it was only natural aircraft would carry them for use against other aircraft. Most AAMs are divided into shorter-ranged infrared homing missiles, such as the Sidewinder and Atoll, and radar homing designs such as the US AMRAAM, UK's Skyflash, or Chines PL-12.

Anti-submarine Missiles provide an ability to fire at a hostile submarine at a distance. The warhead is a torpedo or sometimes depth charge. The missile carries the warhead to the estimated location of the submarine, where it separates and floats down to the water on a parachute. Once in the water the torpedo begins searching for the target.

Cruise Missiles combine long range with a heavy warhead. They typically fly low and have guidance systems similar to the LAM. They can be subsonic, supersonic and some recent designs are capable of hypersonic (Mach 5+) speeds.

Ballistic Missiles have high trajectories, often entering suborbital space. Ranges can vary from less than 100 miles for battlefield use to intercontinental weapons with ranges up to 18,000 miles. They can be land, submarine or aircraft launched. While most often thought of as nuclear armed, they can carry conventional warheads. China's DF-21 missile is touted as the world's first anti-ship ballistic missile and a threat to US Navy carrier strike groups.

Anti-satellite Missiles (ASATs) target an enemy's ability to observe and communicate using space assets. The United States, China, Russia and India have all demonstrated the ability to successfully employ ASATs. The US Navy did so using an SM-3 missile launched from a destroyer in 2008.

LEFT: The Japanese guided missile patrol craft *Wakataka* fires a domestically produced Type 90 anti-ship missile. The weapon is equivalent to the US Harpoon missile. Japanese Government

NAVAL AIRPOWER

Carrier aircraft and coastal protection

ABOVE: F-14 Tomcats on the flight deck of USS *Harry Truman* in 2005. The F-14 is perhaps the most famous US carrier-based fighter and flew its final missions over Iraq and Afghanistan. US DoD

Airpower is vital for modern warfare in general. In naval warfare, aircraft are indeed a 'game-changer,' providing new threats and opportunities. Aircraft allow a nation without a strong navy to protect their coastline and keep enemy forces at a distance. They also allow navies with aircraft carriers to strike far inland, putting more than just the coast at risk of attack. Several types of aircraft figure prominently in naval operations.

Carrier aircraft are the most significant technology to increase naval combat power in the last century. From their humble origins in the reconnaissance and gunnery spotting roles of the 1920s and early 1930s, aircraft quickly evolved into formidable weapons in their own right, carried by a new type of warship, the aircraft carrier. Initially developed as either fighters for protection or attack aircraft for delivering bombs and torpedoes and scouting, they have evolved into multi-role aircraft able to do all three.

Further, specialised planes for anti-submarine, electronic warfare, early warning and command and control missions increase the capabilities of navies possessing carriers able to operate them. During the Falklands crisis (see page 62), the British carrier task force could operate Harrier fighters and anti-submarine helicopters but were hampered by their lack of electronic warfare and early warning aircraft, such as the US EA-6B Prowler and E-2C Hawkeye, respectively. The absence was partially made up for through using Hawker Siddeley Nimrod maritime patrol planes operating at extreme distance using tanker support. However, having such aircraft available to the task force would have made force protection much easier, possibly avoiding some of the losses taken.

Vertical/Short Take Off and Landing (V/STOL) designs, such as the Harrier and modern F-35B, can be operated from much smaller carriers, a less expensive option. Many nations operate them from

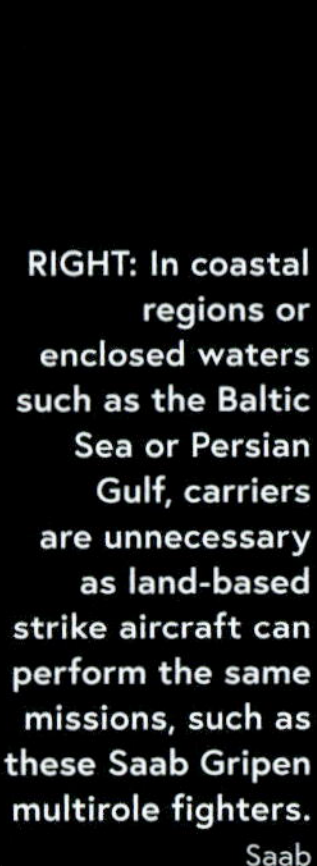

RIGHT: In coastal regions or enclosed waters such as the Baltic Sea or Persian Gulf, carriers are unnecessary as land-based strike aircraft can perform the same missions, such as these Saab Gripen multirole fighters. Saab

ships originally designed only to operate helicopters, though the flight decks must be reinforced to handle the heat generated by a V/STOL plane during take-off and landing.

Helicopters are the most versatile aircraft in any naval inventory, though often not the most capable in any particular role. Often regarded mainly for their cargo, search and rescue, transport and anti-submarine capabilities, helicopters can also function very effectively as strike aircraft in the right circumstances; several of the battle accounts in this edition include helicopters performing strike missions.

A trend seen more often in the last decade involves training army helicopter pilots to operate their aircraft from naval vessels. This can increase their range and allow them to operate much farther out to sea. The Royal Navy and USN, for example, regularly train with AH64 Apache attack helicopter units. This would also allow army helicopters to transit great distances, such as between islands in the Pacific, by allowing them to refuel aboard ships.

Land-Based Aircraft can include everything from helicopters to fighter/strike planes, bombers and patrol planes, operated by navies or air forces. They carry out the same missions, only limited by their access to tankers allowing them to operate farther from the coast. Depending on numbers available, this could allow mass strikes against approaching enemy naval forces. Since much larger planes can operate from bases ashore, they can have much more range and endurance than carrier planes.

RIGHT: Helicopters are often overlooked as maritime strike aircraft but can be a real threat to warships which lack proper air defences. This Mexican Navy helicopter fires rockets at a decommissioned US destroyer during a sinking exercise. US Navy

RIGHT: An American F-18 Hornet lands on the French carrier *Charles De Gaulle*. This ship is one of only a few non-US carriers that can operate regular fixed-wing aircraft. US Navy

BELOW: Maritime patrol planes such as this Kawasaki P-1, seen here dropping chaff, are true multi-role aircraft, with anti-submarine, anti-ship and reconnaissance capabilities. JMSDF

Combat missions at sea require specialised training, not always provided to air force pilots, however. During the Falklands crisis, the Argentine Air Force strike pilots had less success against the ships of the Royal Navy because they received little training in making attacks on moving targets. For most air forces, maritime missions are secondary.

Unmanned Aerial Systems (UAS) have actually been operationally active since the 1960s but made rapid improvement in the last 30 years. Initially used for reconnaissance, UAS – commonly referred to as drones – have expanded into strike missions as well, seeing much use in that role in the last two decades. As the technology rapidly advances, new designs will assume many other roles. See page 92 for a summary of future UAS capabilities and missions.

TORPEDOES

Subsurface ship and submarine killer

RIGHT: An Anti-submarine Rocket (ASROC) flashes from a vertical launch tube of USS *Pinckney*. The rocket's warhead is a MK46 torpedo. US Navy

Self-propelled naval torpedoes first appeared in the mid-1800s. During that period, the term torpedo was often applied to what would today be called mines, including land mines. Torpedoes provided an advantage to smaller navies as they could be mounted on smaller vessels and posed a threat to the large, armoured warships of the period. The modern warship classification destroyer originated as 'torpedo boat destroyer,' as it was intended to defend large warships from attack by small, agile torpedo boats.

As technology advanced in the 20th century, torpedoes were adapted for use first on submarines, then on aircraft, increasing the danger of air attack on warships. Many surface warships continued to carry torpedoes, particularly smaller vessels such as destroyers, for which the torpedo comprised its primary armament against larger capital ships. After World War Two aircraft ceased to carry torpedoes for anti-ship use, as helicopters and patrol aircraft began carrying them in the anti-submarine role. Surface ships still carry them primarily for anti-submarine work as well; while the torpedoes can target surface ships, their short range compared to modern missiles would require a surface ship to get much closer for an attack.

The first torpedoes lacked guidance, running on a straight ballistic course until it struck a target or reached the limit of its range. Torpedoes using acoustic, wake-homing and wire guidance also exist. Unguided torpedoes, many of them left over from World War Two, remained in use through much of the postwar era, notably used in the Falklands conflict (see page 62). As submarines became much faster and deeper diving during the Cold War, torpedoes similarly improved in speed and depth.

RIGHT: A decommissioned French warship suffers a hit from a French F21 heavy torpedo during testing in 2024. French Navy

BELOW: A Royal Navy Wildcat helicopter drops a training torpedo during an exercise in Norway, 2025. The torpedo is recoverable for reuse. UK MoD Crown Copyright

Some designs still explode through impacting the target directly although many powerful new designs explode under the ship, lifting it and stressing the hull. A cavity is created in the water under the ship, which then 'falls' into it, further stressing the ship's centre. Next, the surge of water rushing in to fill the cavity strikes the hull; together, these effects are enough to cripple or sink most ships.

Torpedoes are the main weapon used in submarine and anti-submarine warfare. Most modern torpedoes can sink or disable an enemy submarine or surface ship with a single hit. Most submarines are equipped with four to eight torpedo tubes. After firing, reloading each tube can take 10-15 minutes, meaning the submarine must hide or retire to reload to avoid counterattack. Surface ships carrying torpedoes usually carry two to six launch tubes which can be reloaded in about the same time.

For anti-submarine work, aircraft-delivered torpedoes are generally equipped with parachutes so they enter the water at a safe velocity. Once in the water their propulsion system activates, and the torpedo begins searching for its target. An attack on a submarine

can disrupt its own attack as it must deploy countermeasures and evade the attack, since a hit virtually guarantees the loss of the submarine and its crew. Aircraft are useful for anti-submarine work as they can search for and drop torpedoes on submarines at a distance from the submarine's target. They are also largely immune from counterattack by a submarine.

Torpedo countermeasures include decoys and jamming devices. Towed arrays are pulled behind the vessel using a cable. Towed arrays imitate the signature of their vessel, causing the incoming torpedo to home on it rather than the target. Each towed array carries a number of decoy devices, allowing them to engage against more than one torpedo. Active countermeasure systems, which use a small torpedo to intercept the incoming weapon, are still in the development stage.

While widely used, torpedoes have only been used three times to sink naval vessels since 1945. In 1971, the Pakistani submarine *Hangor* sank the Indian frigate *Khukri* (see page 42). HMS *Conqueror* sank the Argentine cruiser *General Belgrano* in 1982 (see page 62). In 2010, a North Korean midget submarine sank the South Korean corvette *Cheonan* using a torpedo.

ABOVE: The USS *John S. McCain* launches a torpedo during an anti-submarine exercise in the Philippine Sea, 2021. Each Arleigh Burke-class destroyer carries two Mark 32 triple torpedo tubes. US Navy

LEFT: An obsolete US submarine is sunk during an exercise by a torpedo launched from USS *Wahoo* in 1968. US Navy

BELOW: A torpedo drops from the ordnance bay of an RAF Poseidon maritime patrol aircraft during an exercise, simulating an attack on an enemy submarine. The Poseidon can carry five torpedoes in its internal bay and up to six more on external hardpoints. UK MoD Crown Copyright

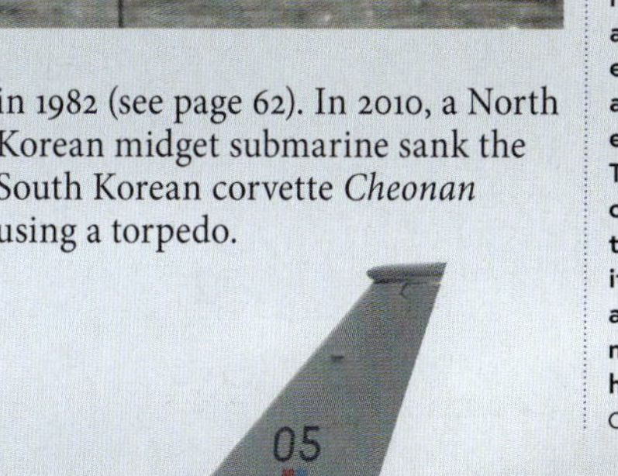

MINE WARFARE

Important but often overlooked

Mines are among the most significant weapons in naval warfare, but they receive little thought or consideration until one blasts open the hull of a warship or merchant vessel. Compared to missiles and aircraft, mines are dull and devious, with a tinge of dishonour about their use. Mines are often an afterthought to major navies, which often neglect their countermine forces until they lose a ship to one. The US Navy (USN) learned this lesson in the Persian Gulf during the 1980s, suffering three ships damaged by mines from 1988 to 1991.

The mine's status as an underhand weapon is belied by its simple effectiveness and significance to naval warfare overall. It is the weapon of weaker powers outmatched by larger ones. They can be effective in denying an area to an enemy, who must proceed cautiously through waters sown with mines. As part of an Anti-Access/Area Denial (A2AD) defence, mines can keep an enemy away from a vital stretch of coastline or channel an enemy into an engagement area.

All four US ships lost in the Korean War were lost to mines and several USN ships suffered damage from Iraqi mines during the 1991 Gulf War. While neither of these cases was a true setback in their respective conflicts, they proved more effective than their nation's warships. Mines are relatively cheap and easy to emplace, allowing a nation to deploy large numbers of them. Larger navies also use mines, although often in more specific circumstances. Mines can be used to block the entrance to an enemy harbour, keeping warships in port and preventing commerce.

An example is the Russian Baltic Fleet at St. Petersburg. It must transit the narrow Gulf of Finland to reach the Baltic Sea. The Gulf can be sown with mines to stop or slow Russian movement. Since it is now flanked by NATO members, a minefield can be covered by shore-based missiles and aircraft. Similarly, the Russians could attempt to mine the Gulf west of the cities of Helsinki and

ABOVE: Mines are a persistent threat. This World War Two-era mine was detonated by a Norwegian team off the German coast in 2016. US Navy

LEFT: The Mine Countermeasures Vessel HMS *Middleton* transiting the Strait of Hormuz. The crew uses sonar, divers and remote vehicles to clear mines. UK MoD Crown Copyright

Tallinn, hindering access to them. Taiwan could use mines in the shallow areas outside their western harbours to slow and degrade an invading Chinese force.

Mines come in several types. The drifting mine is the stereotype (the classic sphere with spike-shaped contact fuses). These mines drift with the current and are the most unpredictable as they could pose a threat to friendly or neutral shipping. They generally explode on contact or via proximity fuse. Moored mines are attached to an anchor by a rope, chain or cord so they will stay in one place. Bottom mines sink to the sea floor and remain in place, equipped with sensors that detect a ship overhead and explode or launch a torpedo. Their fuses detect a ship's magnetism, sense its noise acoustically, or react to changes in water pressure. An observer can also detonate mines remotely.

Modern mines can be delivered by ships, submarines and aircraft. Many designs now self-destruct after a given period to avoid persistent hazards to navigation. Mines from both world wars are still occasionally encountered even in the 2020s. Their deteriorated state makes them even more dangerous to eliminate.

Clearing mines requires specially trained sailors and equipment. Increasingly, robotic and remotely controlled systems are used to lower the risk. A simple method for warships which spot a nearby mine is to engage them with the ship's guns. Loitering munitions and small drones, widely used in the Ukraine War, show promise as they can target a mine with great precision.

Just as small, inexpensive munitions are gaining wide use on land, adding cheap guidance and sensor technologies to naval mines is increasing their lethality and versatility. The USN uses the Quickstrike series of air-dropped mines, which are based on the Mk. 80 family of 500lb, 1000lb and 2,000lb aircraft bombs. These weapons are effective in shallow water and use a fuse which detects passing ships. Upgraded versions have a GPS guidance system or fold out wings so the aircraft can deploy it from a greater distance. The US also uses the Mk 67 Submarine Launched Mobile Mine (SLMM) which can be used in deeper water. Upon detecting a target this mine launches a torpedo with a 330lb explosive warhead.

ABOVE: A US Navy officer checks a MK-65 Quickstrike mine carried on a P-3 Orion maritime patrol aircraft. The Quickstrike is an air-dropped mine for use in shallow water. US Navy

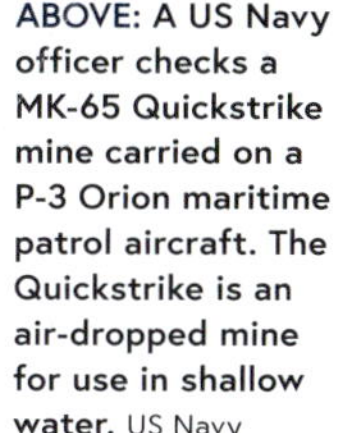

LEFT: US and Japanese sailors during a mine countermeasures exercise; here they are attaching explosives to a dummy mine to destroy it. US Navy

LEFT: Warships will engage nearby mines with their onboard close defence weapons. Here the destroyer USS *Delbert D. Black* uses a 25mm cannon during countermine training in the Atlantic Ocean. US Navy

THE FRENCH NAVY IN VIETNAM

The creation of modern riverine warfare 1946-54

In the aftermath of World War Two, several European powers moved to reassert their control over colonies which had been occupied by Axis powers due to Nazi occupation of the home nations. The Japanese Empire occupied Vietnam from September 1940 until its surrender in August 1945. Afterward French forces arrived to reassume control of the country.

This was unacceptable to the Viet Minh, led by Ho Chi Minh, who led resistance against the Japanese during the war, with considerable aid from the Allies. However, the movement was communist, unacceptable to the Allied powers after the war, when the next conflict was shaping into the struggle between democracy and communism. The initial French commitment to Vietnam was numerically insufficient to regain control of the country, a vast nation of plains, jungles, mountains and rivers. The French received limited military aid from the British and Americans and gradually committed more of its forces to defeating the Viet Minh.

The military situation moved back and forth in a pattern which in many ways resembled the later and better-known American experience in Vietnam in the 1960s. The Viet Minh could easily control the countryside, retreating when faced with superior firepower and returning when the French inevitably withdrew. The French lacked the manpower to be strong everywhere and so had to choose when and where to act. They could control the towns and cities and generally succeeded in driving out any Viet Minh attack on such population centres. The French ruled the day while the Viet Minh ruled the night. Each side had notable successes and failures.

As the Americans learned a decade later, one key to defeating the Viet Minh was mobility. Helicopters were still a new and immature technology and could not be counted on to move large numbers of troops. On land, French troops used armour and vehicles to move and attack in force, but roads limit where a force

BELOW: French-operated M24 Chaffee tanks embark on a Landing Ship, Utility (LSU) for transport in 1954. US Navy

can operate and are susceptible to ambush. Vietnam is also a nation of rivers and waterways, however, with much of its trade, food production and transport making use of them. The Mekong Delta alone covers 26,000 square miles with 2,750 miles of inland waterways. To exploit the potential of naval and amphibious forces to use the rivers and coastline, the French developed a potent force to carry out fast operations and achieve surprise.

The Division d'Infanterie Navale d'Assaut, or 'Naval Assault Division', is better known by its abbreviation 'dinassaut.' Initially, French naval forces in Vietnam used leftover barges, junks and other small craft, supported by a few warships off the coast. Over time these forces expanded into several dinassauts spread across the country. In the late 1940s the first shipments of surplus World War Two amphibious assault ships and landing craft arrived, the first provided by the British. Some aid arrived from the United States and the amount increased dramatically once the Korean War began in 1950, as the West began to fear the spread of communism across Asia. More naval vessels arrived over the next few years and eventually ten dinassauts were formed.

A typical squadron-sized dinassaut operated 12 to 18 craft, though in practice these numbers varied due to availability and combat losses. A lieutenant usually commanded, and while technically the title »

LEFT: The flight deck of *Arromanches* in 1951, with Helldiver dive bombers lined up to one side and Hellcat fighters on the other. These aircraft could be very effective against the Viet Minh. US Navy

LEFT: French naval commandos come ashore on the coast of Annam, 1950. Their ability to quickly move to critical points surprised the Viet Minh on several occasions. NARA

BELOW: The light carrier *Arromanches* and destroyer *Le Malan* sail into Da Nang Bay, October 1951. The Viet Minh had nothing with which to threaten a carrier while offshore. US Navy

LEFT: The light carrier *La Fayette* sailing in Vietnamese waters, 1953. Note the Sikorsky helicopter just forward of the carrier's island. US Navy

LEFT: A Grumman Goose observation plane flies over a French river gunboat in 1954. Aircraft and dinassaut vessels cooperated in spotting and engaging enemy positions along the rivers. US Navy

dinassaut belonged to the entire force as a whole, each individual squadron also went by the name dinassaut. Amphibious and landing craft proved ideal, as they could be armed with powerful weapons and armoured to a degree. Their shallow drafts allowed them to traverse waterways even at low tide or in dry seasons when the water's depth dropped dramatically.

Dinassauts operated in four distinct groups. The Opening Group acted as a reconnaissance and patrol formation. It possessed monitors armed with 40mm cannon, machine guns and 81mm or 120mm mortars. These craft were converted LCMs (Landing Craft, Mechanised). The French fitted some monitors and other craft with tank turrets, rocket launchers and flamethrowers. The opening group used its heavy firepower to suppress the enemy while the rest of the dinassaut moved to land troops or launch their own attacks.

The Command Group used larger vessels, such as LSSLs (Landing Ship Supply, Large), allowing better command and control of the force in action. These small ships could accommodate the radio equipment needed to call in artillery and air support. They often carried a 76mm cannon along with 40mm and 20mm weapons. The Transport Group used LCMs to carry troops for landing operations. Each could carry about a platoon of infantry and sometimes carried tanks or trucks. A company of French naval commandos typically operated with each dinassaut, though army paratroopers and regular infantry were also used, depending on mission.

For larger operations, several dinassauts would operate together. During these missions, the ground force might expand to several battalions. The French naval commandos were later joined by Vietnamese commandos who proved effective in action. Dinassauts depended on firepower and the added armour of their craft to survive combat, since they had no cover when operating on a river and could be fired on from either or both banks. French Marine Col Victor Croizat explained: "For these craft to serve on inland waters they had to be armoured to withstand the shock of surprise encounters at short ranges. They also needed substantial armament to deliver promptly the heavy volume of fire to counter an ambush. Armament, moreover, had to include a mix of high and flat trajectory weapons to ensure that all types of targets along the waterways and over the riverbanks could be taken under fire."

The first operations of the dinassauts took the Viet Minh by surprise, as they expected the French to use roads. However, the Viet Minh learned quickly and prepared

BELOW: Two French LCVPs (Landing Craft, Vehicle/Personnel) commonly used by dinassauts. Note the added weapons and armour plating. US Navy

ambushes along the waterways whenever possible. They frequently used machine guns and bazookas to attack dinassauts as they moved toward their objectives, which caused casualties but rarely disabled a vessel. Mines became their preferred weapon for damaging watercraft, though they could be difficult to employ given the seasonally changing river conditions. In response, the dinassauts employed minesweepers.

Notable dinassaut actions include:

Nam Dinh, 1946: A dinassaut deployed to this city to relieve its garrison, under heavy attack. After fighting through several ambushes, the dinassaut approached the city using the Bamboo Canal. Another ambush sprung, this time from both sides of the canal. The French commander died almost immediately, but his second in command noticed the enemy fire was heavier from the bank opposite their intended landing point. He ordered the dinassaut to land on the opposite bank, where they quickly overwhelmed the Viet Minh before turning their attention to the other side of the canal. Those Viet Minh soon retreated, and the French completed their mission.

Operation Foudre, 1951: As part of a response to a Viet Minh offensive, a reinforced dinassaut arrived at the town of Ninh Binh just as the Viet Minh entered the town and set up defences. An LSSL used its 76mm gun to blast the town's watchtower, where the Viet Minh had concentrated some troops. This completely disorganised the defence, and the French troops landed to recapture the town took 55 prisoners from the watchtower alone.

LEFT: A river monitor leads a dinassaut deep into Vietnamese territory, 1954. Note the tank turret installed for firepower and the exposed position of the lookout. US Navy

Operation Lorraine, 1952: Two dinassauts advanced up several rivers to cut off Viet Minh supply routes as part of a large operation by ground troops. They initially transported troops to staging areas and later landed naval commandos and Moroccan colonial infantry to engage Viet Minh forces. The Viet Minh underestimated the dinassaut's ability to quickly move troops to critical points.

While the dinassauts prowled the rivers and coastline, other French naval forces also played their part. In particular, French aircraft carriers proved vital in providing the ground forces with effective air support. The escort carrier *Dixmude* (formerly HMS *Biter*) used US-built Dauntless dive bombers between 1945 and 1949, providing mobile firepower. The carrier *Arromanches* (formerly HMS *Colossus*) employed a mix of fighters and dive bombers during her 1948 deployment to Vietnam.

In 1951 France received the light carrier USS *Langley*, taken from reserve and transferred under a military aid programme. Renamed the *La Fayette*, she was joined in 1953 by the *Bois Belleau* (former USS *Belleau Wood*). Both saw service in Vietnamese waters. During the last phase of the war, during the fighting at Dien Bien Phu, carrier aircraft had trouble reaching the battle area due to its distance from the coast. Several squadrons went ashore to operate at land bases, as the superior training of the naval pilots proved vital to flying in the often-poor weather over the battlefield. General Henri Navarre later said the French naval air arm was the only military arm which consistently met all its obligations during this final period of the war.

While France lost its war in Vietnam for a number of reasons, the performance of its navy stands out, particularly the dinassauts. They set the example for riverine and coastal operations which inform theories of such warfare to this day.

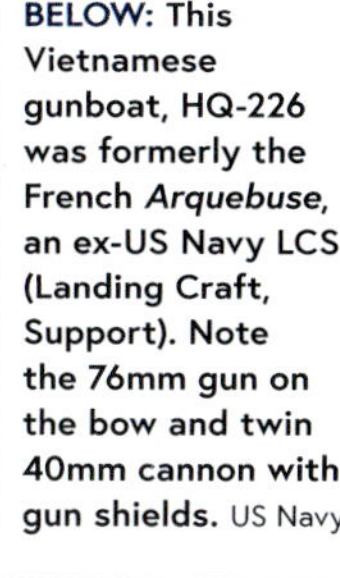

BELOW: This Vietnamese gunboat, HQ-226 was formerly the French *Arquebuse*, an ex-US Navy LCS (Landing Craft, Support). Note the 76mm gun on the bow and twin 40mm cannon with gun shields. US Navy

BATTLE ON THE YANGTZE

HMS *Amethyst*, 1949

After World War Two ended, trade routes began to reopen in China and Britain employed naval vessels to combat piracy and protect their embassies and interests in the region. This mission became more precarious as the nationalist and communist Chinese factions renewed the conflict they had tentatively put on hold during the war. The conflict quickly turned against the nationalists and the communists advanced throughout the country.

By April 1949, the fighting had reached the Yangtze River between Shanghai and Nanking, the waterway used by the small warships that the Royal Navy deployed to secure the route between the two cities. On April 20, HMS *Amethyst*, a Black Swan-class frigate armed with six 4in guns and a pair each of 20mm and 40mm cannon, proceeded up the Yangtze toward Nanking to relieve HMS *Concord* as the guard ship there. The nationalists occupied the south bank of the river while the communists occupied the north. *Amethyst* flew a number of British flags to mark her as neutral, but the crew stood ready for trouble.

The ship took fire along the route and when it reached Rose Island an artillery battery opened an accurate fire on her. Some small boats lay anchored in a nearby creek, to be used by the communists for the eventual assault crossing. *Amethyst's* captain, Lt Cdr B. Skinner, ordered full ahead and angled the ship toward the nationalist side to open the range. Several shells struck the wheelhouse, killing or wounding all inside. Skinner ordered his first lieutenant, George Weston, to return fire. As soon as he gave the order two more shells hit the bridge, mortally wounding Skinner. Weston took a shell splinter in the chest but took command despite the terrible pain. Before he could correct the ship's turn, it ran aground, stern toward the enemy.

Weston sent a radio message to Nanking and ordered the aft turret to fire on local control. It put out a steady fire until knocked out by a direct hit. Soon dead and wounded sailors covered the deck and two of *Amethyst*'s medical personnel were killed. Weston evacuated as many of his wounded as possible to Rose Island under steady enemy machine gun fire. The ship lost 22 dead and 31 wounded. The artillery stopped afterward but machine gun fire continued to strike *Amethyst* while belowdecks the crew worked to restore power and lighten the ship.

The destroyer HMS *Consort* responded to *Amethyst*'s radio call from Nanking. Flying numerous British flags and steaming at 30 knots, *Consort* was nevertheless fired upon by the communists.

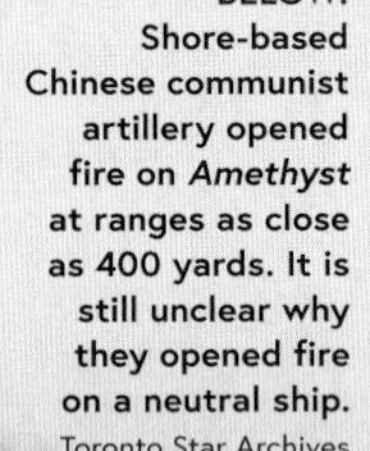

BELOW: Shore-based Chinese communist artillery opened fire on *Amethyst* at ranges as close as 400 yards. It is still unclear why they opened fire on a neutral ship.
Toronto Star Archives

The destroyer returned fire, destroyed one Chinese battery and attempted to tow *Amethyst* free from the shallows. However, the Chinese deployed anti-tank guns and put such a heavy fire on *Consort* she had to retire or risk being disabled. The destroyer took 56 hits and suffered 33 casualties. After midnight, *Amethyst* succeeded in getting free and sailed four miles upstream to a slightly safer location. The nationalist Chinese evacuated the ship's wounded.

The next morning the cruiser *London* and frigate *Black Swan* sailed from Shanghai to relieve *Amethyst* and fought a protracted gunnery duel with the communist guns. Despite causing heavy damage themselves, the two ships were large and easy to hit. After firing over 2,500 rounds, the two ships had to retire before reaching *Amethyst*. The RAF managed to land a replacement medical officer using a Sunderland flying boat and *Amethyst* moved twice more to avoid further enemy fire, eventually settling at Ta Sha Island, as it lacked cover for the enemy's troops.

As Lt Weston was badly wounded, Lt Cdr John Kerans, an assistant naval attaché from the British Embassy, drove to the ship and assumed command. He conducted a funeral for the ship's dead and prepared the ship for scuttling in case escape proved impossible. Further rescue attempts were impractical for the moment and the ship was too damaged to risk moving alone. Soon the nationalists withdrew from the area under a renewed communist offensive and a series of negotiations with the communists ensued. The Chinese refrained from further attacks but refused to allow *Amethyst* to leave. They did allow the crew to purchase supplies, though at exorbitant prices.

By July, however, the situation aboard ship became steadily more difficult, food and water were rationed and restrictions were imposed on fuel use. Soon, there would not be enough fuel to get away. However, the fighting had moved away and fewer Chinese guns lay near the river. The morale of *Amethyst*'s crew remained high, so Kerans sent a message that he intended to break out at 10pm on July 30. His superiors assured Kerans they would support his judgement. The crew prepared to sail, making final, hasty repairs and greasing the anchor line so it would slip silently. They also applied sheeting and paint to make *Amethyst* appear similar to a Chinese ship.

As the time neared, Kerans chose to delay a few minutes while some approaching clouds obscured the moon. As *Amethyst* waited, a Chinese refugee ship, the *Kiang Lin Liberation*, appeared, sailing toward Shanghai. Kerans used the civilian freighter to cover his movement and then followed it, which helped with navigation as the British lacked good charts of the river.

All went smoothly for a half hour, until the Chinese freighter received a challenge from a shore battery, a flare overhead. It responded with a coded blast from its siren. Another flare flew to challenge *Amethyst*, and when no reply came an armed landing craft appeared to investigate. The landing craft fired a machine gun across *Amethyst*'s bow, but the rounds struck the communist battery, which opened fire. *Amethyst* replied with machine guns and cannon. Kerans also ordered the engine room to make smoke as the ship took several hits. In the confusion, however, the communists fired into the freighter and their own landing craft.

Amethyst increased speed to 22kts. Two hours later the ship passed a former nationalist naval base at Kiang Yin. A boat and a shore battery opened fire, but to little effect. Just ahead lay a line of sunken ships placed across the river in 1937 during the war with Japan. Two flashing buoys were supposed to »

ABOVE: HMS *London* after the rescue attempt. The damage from shell hits is visible. Official Photo

LEFT: HMS *Amethyst* docked at Hong Kong after her escape from the Yangtze River. A shell hole in her lower stern is evident. IWM HU129713

mark the passage through, but only one was operational. Kerans chose to pass close to starboard and *Amethyst* got through.

Ahead lay a final obstacle, two forts at Woosung and Par Shan. Each had 6in guns which could easily sink the British vessel. The destroyer *Concord* lay nearby, prepared to give support if the forts opened fire and as *Amethyst* approached, the crew saw the two fort's searchlights moving across the water ahead. Kerans ordered full speed ahead and sailed through. Though at least one light swept over the ship, the forts did not open fire and *Amethyst* made it to sea. The time was 05:29; it took a little over seven hours to get free after more than three months of effective captivity. *Concord* joined *Amethyst* as both sailed away from the mouth of the Yangtze.

Kerens immediately sent a signal: "Have rejoined the fleet south of Woosung. No damage. No casualties. God save the King!" The crew received a hero's welcome when the ship arrived in Hong Kong for repairs. Congratulations poured in from around the world and on returning to England, the entire crew received an audience with King George VI. In 1957 the movie The Yangtse Incident premiered in theatres, filmed aboard *Amethyst*. Within a few months, however, the ship went to the scrapper's yard, her service at an end.

ABOVE: A portrait of *Amethyst* arriving at Hong Kong on August 3, 1949. After escaping, sailors from HMS *Concord* transferred aboard to relieve the exhausted crew. Royal Museums Greenwich

LEFT: A view of HMS *Amethyst* from World War Two. During the war she sank one German submarine and assisted in the destruction of another. IWM A30156

LEFT: *Amethyst*'s crew patched holes above the waterline using mattresses held in place by timbers. These repairs proved enough to get the ship to safety. IWM HU45375

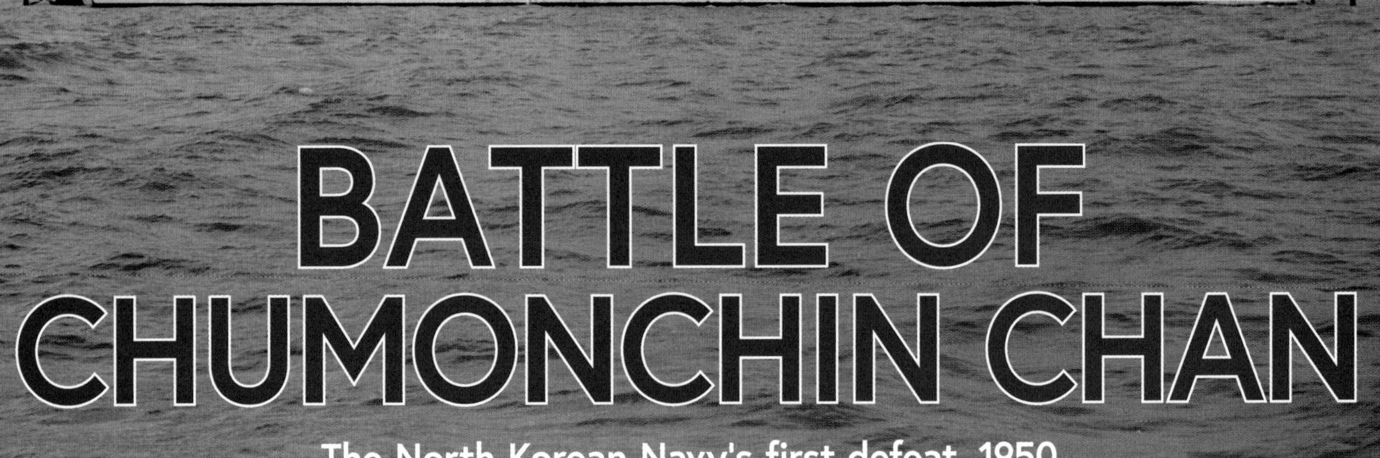

BATTLE OF CHUMONCHIN CHAN

The North Korean Navy's first defeat, 1950

When North Korea invaded its southern neighbour in June 1950, it took the West by surprise. The North Korean People's Army (NKPA), equipped with 200 T-34 tanks and heavy artillery, quickly overwhelmed the lightly armed South Korean military, which was still being organised and trained, primarily by American advisors. Within a few days the NKPA reached Seoul, the South Korean capital, and continued south, threatening to occupy the entire Korean Peninsula unless quick action was taken. The situation seemed dire.

The United Nations did prove quick to respond, though initially it had few forces on hand to do so with. Most of what was available came from the United States and United Kingdom, though many other nations contributed forces in the coming months. Unfortunately, even the Americans and British were hard pressed to provide substantial forces immediately. Both had demobilised their militaries at the end of World War Two, and subsequent budget cuts had severe effects on personnel, training and equipment. The closest US Army troops were on occupation duty in Japan, but their standards of training had lapsed, and they lacked heavy weapons. Better-equipped units were quickly organised in the United States, but it would take time for them to arrive by sea.

Both the Royal Navy (RN) and United States Navy (USN) had ships deployed in the region and these were quickly ordered to Korea. One advantage naval forces possess is that it takes much the same skills to operate a ship in peacetime as in wartime, giving them a generally higher level of overall readiness. Ships operating in the Western Pacific during this period also had to contend with the Chinese civil war and French counterinsurgency operations in Vietnam in addition to the general chaos due to the end of World War Two and subsequent withdrawal of Japanese forces. This compelled preparedness to even higher levels as these ships sailed Pacific waters carrying out the wishes of their governments.

Once in the area, these British and American ships formed ad hoc task forces, holding the line until additional warships could arrive. While the bulk of the fighting took place on land, that land mass was a peninsula, allowing warships to range along them, placing considerable territory within range on their guns.

Additionally, islands and peninsulas make wide use of coastal waterways to move cargo cheaply and the Korean Peninsula was no different. The North Koreans used small craft to move ammunition, food and supplies quickly to their advancing ground troops. UN naval vessels could interdict this coastal traffic, denying the North Koreans the use of the sea as a resupply line. The British and US navies possessed experience doing this during World War Two, when they had effectively stripped Japanese coastal waters of all intercoastal shipping, greatly reducing Japan's ability to move food and industrial output to where it was needed. These UN forces could do so again off the shores of Korea. »

ABOVE: USS *Juneau* in 1952. Her six 5in gun turrets can be clearly seen and were capable of firing 15 rounds per minute from each gun to a range of 17,000 yards. US Navy

ABOVE: A grainy image of a Soviet-built gunboat similar to those used by the tiny North Korean Navy. These small and lightly armed craft proved no match for British and American warships. US Navy

RIGHT: A G-5 torpedo boat in Soviet Service. At least five served in the North Korean Navy, with three lost at Chumonchin Chan. Russian Archives

When the war began the light cruiser HMS *Jamaica* and frigate HMS *Black Swan* were in transit from Hong Kong to Japan. The 8,700-ton *Jamaica* carried a dozen 6in (152mm) guns in four triple turrets along with eight 4in (102mm) guns in twin turrets. Her escort, the 1,250 ton *Black Swan*, carried six 4in guns in twin turrets. Both ships saw extensive service in World War Two, where *Jamaica* helped sink the German battlecruiser *Scharnhorst* in December 1943. *Black Swan* escorted convoys, rescued survivors of the cargo ship *Empire Star* and helped sink a German U-boat in 1943. The ship also saw action in the rescue attempt of HMS *Amethyst* the year before (see page 22).

Diverted to Korea, both ships soon joined with the USN light cruiser USS *Juneau* (CL-119), an 8,400 ton anti-aircraft ship bearing a dozen 5in (127mm) cannon in six twin turrets. *Juneau* was a new ship, commissioned in February 1946. When the war began the ship served as the flagship of rear Admiral J.M. Higgins. On 29 June *Juneau* carried out a bombardment of North Korean shore installations before joining forces with *Jamaica* and *Black Swan*.

On the morning of July 2, 1950, the three ships operated off the eastern coast of South Korea, just south of the 38th Parallel, the official border between North and South Korea. At 06:15 a lookout on *Black Swan* spotted a convoy of North Korean small craft near Chumonchin Chan, heading north. All three ships closed the range to engage the enemy force.

The North Korean convoy consisted of 16 vessels. Ten were trawlers used to carry ammunition to the troops ashore. The six escorts included four torpedo boats, numbered 21 to 24, and two gunboats. All six were Soviet craft from World War Two. The G-5 torpedo boats displaced just under 18 tons, could reach speeds of 53kts and carried a pair of 21in torpedoes and a pair of 12.7mm machine guns. The gunboats were possibly MO-class boats displacing 50 tons and carrying machine guns and up to two 45mm cannon.

As the UN warships closed the distance, the North Korean escorts turned and attacked while the trawlers continued north. They had already unloaded their cargoes and were returning to port. The six North Korean boats were badly outgunned by any one of the UN ships, although a successful torpedo attack could easily have sunk even the light cruisers. Such an attack was the only way to cover the withdrawal of the trawlers, however.

The cruisers opened fire at 11,000 yards, with the North Korean boats closing as fast as possible. The Allied fire proved accurate and deadly. By the time the range dwindled to 4,000 yards, only one of the torpedo boats remained operational, No.21,

BELOW: HMS *Jamaica* during World War Two. During the Korean war she earned the nickname 'Galloping Ghost of the North Korean Coast' as the ship was claimed sunk by the North Koreans at least three times. IWM FL10556

LEFT: HMS *Black Swan* at anchor in 1945. The ship saw extensive service in the Pacific before and during the Korean War. IWM FL2274

which retreated north. No.22 lay dead in the water; No.23 made for the shore to beach before sinking and No.24 had already slipped beneath the waves. Within minutes both gunboats went down as well, blasted by the combined cannon fire of the three UN ships.

New Zealand Navy Midshipman Michael Muschamp served aboard *Jamaica* during the engagement and later relayed his observation of the short battle when the ship went to action stations: "A very perturbed 18-year-old donned clothes, anti-flash gear, and a tin hat in triple quick time. I made my way to my action station on the bridge…I soon saw what all the fuss was about. There were six small craft, trapped between UN three warships and the shore, firing what appeared to be 20mm and 40mm cannon at *Juneau* and *Jamaica*. The two cruisers got the range of the craft and sank four within ten minutes. Another ran ashore in flames and the sixth escaped seaward."

Jamaica rescued several North Korean sailors from the water and interrogated them via a South Korean liaison officer. According to Muschamp's account, when asked why the North Koreans had not fired torpedoes, the prisoners replied they hadn't learned how to fire them yet; their Soviet advisors were supposed to teach them the following week.

The trawlers made their escape, but *Juneau* found and sank them all a few days later. The day after the battle, *Black Swan* took minor damage from a North Korean air attack. The North Koreans later claimed their torpedo boats sank the heavy cruiser USS *Baltimore* during the battle. Torpedo Boat No.21 is on display in Pyongyang with a display to that effect.

However, at the time of the battle *Baltimore* sat in mothballs as part of the US reserve fleet in Bremerton, Washington. It was recommissioned in November 1951. Despite the claimed victory, the North Korean navy generally declined combat with UN warships during the rest of the war.

BELOW: USS *Juneau* at sea in 1951. Her crew is on deck in dress uniform, making this a planned photograph. US Navy

THE KOREAN WAR 1950–53

The West's first test against communist expansion

ABOVE: A US navy minesweeper detonates a North Korean mine off the peninsula's west coast near Nampo, March 1953. UN naval forces were vastly superior, leaving mines as one of North Korea's few effective weapons at sea. US Navy

On the morning of June 25, 1950, 89,000 North Korean troops attacked South Korea, routing its small, poorly trained and ill-equipped army and quickly pushing south. The North Koreans were armed by the Soviet Union and partially trained by Soviet advisors. Everywhere the North Koreans seemed to advance, with little to stand in their way.

One small bright spot came on June 26, before dawn. The small South Korean's Navy's most capable ship, the patrol ship *Bak Du San,* left the base at Chinhae on a patrol. A former US submarine chaser, the ship carried a 3in gun and six .50-calibre machine guns. About 18 miles from the port of Pusan, the crew spotted another ship in the darkness. The unidentified ship did not respond to signals and when *Bak Du San's* crew aimed its searchlight at the steamer, machine gun fire lashed out, killing the helmsman.

The South Koreans opened fire as the steamer, actually a hijacked former US transport vessel, tried to escape. *Bak Du San* pursued, sinking the enemy ship and killing almost all the 600 North Korean troops aboard. The North Koreans were apparently trying to seize Pusan; had they succeeded, UN forces would have lacked the fallback position they used to blunt the North Korean advance on land. Though a small battle, it carried importance for the war and South Korean naval tradition. It was the first naval battle of the Korean War and is now known as the Battle of the Korea Strait.

The North Korean Navy proved inadequate against UN forces and its few ships soon took refuge in Soviet and Chinese ports, conceding the seas to the UN. While this allowed

RIGHT: HMS *Triumph* operated alongside USS *Valley Forge* during the summer of 1950, providing much needed strike capability for UN forces ashore. US Navy

UN naval forces to concentrate on supporting the ground war, they still had to conduct extensive naval operations. The US and British navies quickly responded to the crisis, along with ships from Australia, Canada, the Netherlands, New Zealand, Thailand and Colombia.

ABOVE: The battleship USS *New Jersey* bombards a target near the 38th Parallel in November 1951. Smoke and dust from the target can be seen at upper left. US Navy

Aircraft Carriers: American, British and Australian aircraft carriers all served during the conflict. They operated a combination of holdover aircraft form World War Two, such as the US Corsair and British Seafire fighters, and newer jet designs such as the US F-9F Panther. Though largely outclassed by the MiG-15, US Navy pilots still managed to shoot down seven of them for the loss of two Panthers.

Close air support of troops in contact became a common mission, as aircraft from a carrier operating close offshore could quickly respond to battlefield situations. Naval aircraft also took part in bombing missions against North Korean industrial and transportation targets, such as bridges.

Naval Gunfire Support: As a peninsula, much of Korea is within range of naval gunfire and everything from battleships to destroyers saw use in shore bombardment. North Korean artillery often fired back, resulting in frequent duels with occasional hits on the UN ships. However, most such engagements went in favour of the UN naval vessels. Cruisers and destroyers were instrumental in hitting North Korean forces around the Pusan Perimeter in August 1950, keeping UN forces on the peninsula. In September, the first US battleship, *Missouri*, arrived; its powerful 16in guns were especially dangerous to the North Koreans. Naval gunfire destroyed a large number of North Korean trains and railroad tracks along with other shore facilities.

Amphibious Landings: UN naval forces carried out one of the most important actions of the war when they landed ground forces at Inchon in September 1950, changing the entire course of the war. Further landings took place later in the war at Wonson and Iwon, the former a preliminary to the fighting at the Chosin Reservoir. At the end of that battle, UN forces were evacuated by sea as well.

Special Operations: The first special operation of the war took place on July 11-12, 1950, when the USN cruiser *Juneau* and destroyer *Mansfield* put a demolition party ashore to blow up a railroad tunnel. The loss of this tunnel cut the rail line from Vladivostok, slowing the delivery of Soviet military aid. Further missions were launched from submarines and small amphibious transports throughout the war. Again, as a peninsula, using ships to move commando forces proved practical.

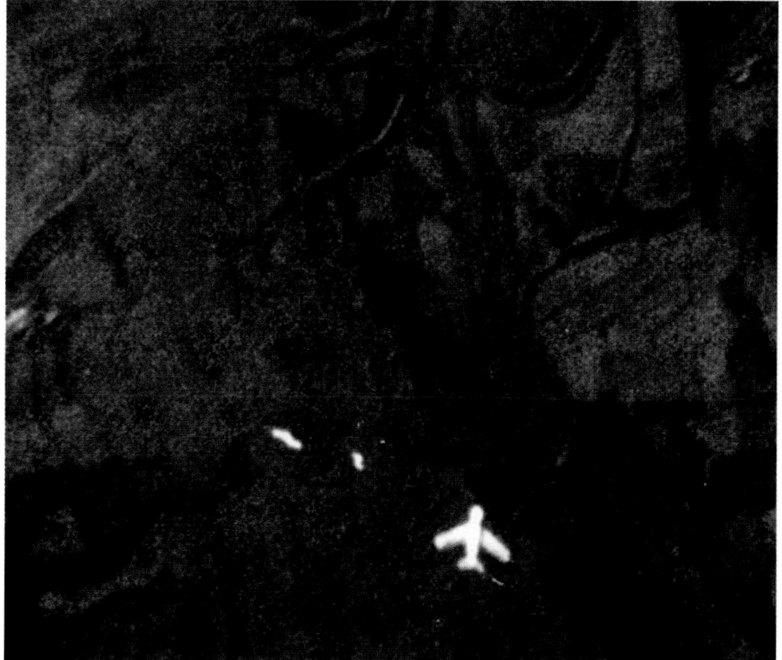

LEFT: A MiG-15 shot down over North Korea by F-9F Panther fighters from USS *Leyte* in November 1950. Carriers played a major role in the air war over Korea. US Navy

Minesweeping: The North Koreans used sea mines to damage UN ships and limit their movement. Most were laid from small boats and sometimes covered by artillery ashore. Minesweepers were soon in demand and brought in from around the world. Notably, 70% of all US Navy casualties in Korea were caused by mines and all four of the US Navy vessels lost in combat during the conflict were to mines.

Blockade: UN ships effectively blockaded North Korea's coast during the conflict. The major port of Wonsan, for example, was the longest naval blockade in modern history, lasting 681 days. Naval attacks effectively destroyed Wonsan, which was not rebuilt until after the war. The blockade limited the ways in which supplies could reach North Korea.

CONFLICT IN THE TAIWAN STRAIT 1954–1958

The origins of an ongoing crisis

When the Chinese Civil War ended in a communist victory, the remaining nationalist forces withdrew from the Chinese mainland to the island of Taiwan. The nationalists managed to retain control of several islands close to the mainland and these became potential flashpoints between the two nations. As these islands are separated from Tiawan by the Taiwan Strait, they are particularly vulnerable to attack by communist forces.

During the 1950s, tensions between the mainland People's Republic of China (PRC) and Taiwanese Republic of China (ROC) simmered, as each feared attack by the other. While today it seems impossible for smaller Taiwan to threaten the PRC, at the time the communists were still consolidating their hold on the nation. China had experienced political instability for decades and the threat of a nationalist-backed uprising loomed large in PRC thinking. As with many previous Chinese regimes, there was no guarantee the communists would retain control, so the possibility of a nationalist return was not unthinkable.

The ROC had a small but capable navy which included a former Royal Navy light cruiser, seven American destroyer escorts and many amphibious landing vessels. The nationalists managed to retain control of nearly all of these ships, while the PRC had almost no navy at the time. PRC plans to invade ROC territory were put on hold when the Korean War began. US President Harry Truman dispatched units of the US 7th Fleet to prevent either side from widening the conflict. The first ships to arrive were the aircraft carrier *Valley Forge*, with destroyers, submarines and support ships. More ships joined later.

The First Taiwan Strait Crisis began in September 1954. PRC forces began heavy artillery bombardment of Jinmen and Mazu Islands, claiming the ROC was launching raids from them. These islands were essential jumping off points for any later invasion of Taiwan. Two American advisors died in the initial barrage and the US response included moving nuclear-capable B-29 bombers to Guam.

While the nuclear threat soon passed after Soviet signals of support

ABOVE: The Gearing-Class destroyer *Herbert J. Thomas* took part in the USN blockade between Taiwan and the Chinese mainland in 1954 and in 1975 was transferred to the Taiwanese Navy through a security assistance programme. She retired in 1999 and was sunk as an artificial reef. USN

LEFT: An F4D-1 Skyray from USS *Lexington* carries Sidewinder missiles during a patrol over the Taiwan Strait in 1958. US Navy

for the PRC, the communists also began air attacks on the Dachen Islands. These islands were not valuable for attacking Taiwan, so they were evacuated with assistance from the 7th Fleet. Afterward, the US and ROC created the Sino-American Mutual Defense Treaty, in which America promised to defend Taiwan. It did not promise to defend the other islands near the coast. The shelling of the islands ceased in May 1955 and the crisis passed for the moment.

A fresh crisis began in July 1958 with aerial engagements over both Taiwan and the mainland. The ROC requested American assistance, including modern weapons such as the then-new Sidewinder infrared homing missile. The US declined to defend the coastal islands but did increase military assistance.

On August 23, the PRC shelled Jinmen with some 40,000 rounds of artillery, some of it directed at incoming supply convoys. The nationalists suffered almost 400 dead and wounded. PRC torpedo boats also sortied, nearly colliding with the destroyer USS *Hopewell*, on patrol in the Strait. Authorised to fire only if attacked, Hopewell's crew stood by while the torpedo boats attacked two ROC landing craft, sinking one and damaging another.

The following day, PRC artillery fire resumed and ROC artillery returned fire. That night several clashes broke out when two groups of PRC gunboats, junks, and amphibious craft attempted a landing. These were driven back by ROC patrol boats. Within a few days USN ships began escorting the convoys, which were not fired at when a US vessel was present.

US military aid included artillery, air defence weapons and numerous fighter aircraft. Secretly, some ROC F-86 Sabres were fitted to carry Sidewinder missiles. The PRC's MiGs had nothing comparable and suffered many losses to the Sidewinder. However, at least one missile failed to explode and became lodged in a MiG-17 which made it back to its base. The recovered missile was given to the Soviets, who reverse-engineered it, producing the AA-2 Atoll missile.

PRC artillery eventually lessened, though it still fired tens of thousands of rounds well into September. The US decided it would defend the islands in this instance, though it knew a determined Chinese assault could only be stopped with nuclear weapons. Planners agreed to use only conventional weapons unless absolutely necessary.

Negotiations went on until the situation slowly improved. At one point the PRC stated they would only fire artillery on even-numbered days if no US ships escorted the convoys. For years both sides continued to fire propaganda shells containing leaflets, with explosives shells fired only in times of political tension. This went on until 1979. A third crisis occurred in 1995-96, and tensions simmer today as the PRC has declared it will eventually reclaim Taiwan. The crises in 1954 – 1958 may prove minor compared to what the future may hold.

ABOVE: The ROC Navy used small patrol craft such as this one, *Tuo Jiang* (PC-104), to escort convoys and defend against Chinese attacks in 1958. ROC Navy

LEFT: A slightly blurry image of a ROC Landing Ship, Tank (LST). These ships were vital in keeping Taiwan's outer islands supplied. US Navy

BELOW: The ROC received extensive US assistance to maintain its naval forces during and after the crises in the 1950s. This is the frigate *Fu Shan*, a former USN ship. US Navy

CUBAN MISSILE CRISIS

The United States and Soviet Union come close to nuclear war

Though the Cuban Missile Crisis of October 1962 did not turn into a conflict, it took the world to the brink of nuclear war. From a maritime perspective, it is an example of a modern naval blockade. A blockade is generally considered an act of war, so the US used the term quarantine to keep the situation peaceful while negotiations continued.

By August of 1962, American intelligence suspected the Soviets were installing nuclear missiles on the island of Cuba. U-2 spy planes first discovered SA-2 anti-aircraft missiles, causing suspicion as to what those weapons were protecting. Confirmation that Soviet short- and intermediate-range nuclear missiles were in Cuba soon reached US President John F. Kennedy. Soviet Leader Nikita Khrushchev denied their existence but had emplaced the missiles to counter the American nuclear weapons in Turkey and NATO's presence in West Berlin.

RIGHT: A P-2H Neptune anti-submarine patrol plane flies over a Soviet freighter during the crisis. This vessel carried disassembled combat aircraft destined for Cuba. US Navy

BELOW: An aerial reconnaissance photograph showing the Soviet missile sites under construction in Cuba. NARA

After considering a range of options, Kennedy chose to blockade Cuba to prevent more Soviet missiles from reaching the island. The United States Navy (USN) received the order to surround the island and prevent offensive weapons from getting through. All US military forces went on high alert.

By mid-October 1962, two shipments of nuclear missiles and 40,000 Soviet troops were in Cuba. These forces included the missile troops as well as air defence and infantry units. USN ships began the quarantine of Soviet and other vessels approaching Cuba. Tensions were high as the navy had to quickly begin an operation it had not prepared to carry out.

One retired USN pilot, then a new lieutenant flying a P-2 anti-submarine plane, recalled being in the region for training when the crisis began. When he reported to the operations centre at his base, a senior officer informed him about the situation, assigned him a patrol area, and told him his plane had been

RIGHT: A USN HSS-1 Seabat anti-submarine helicopter hovers over a Soviet Foxtrot-class submarine during the quarantine operation. The diesel-electric submarines suffered from poor maintenance and habitability during the crisis. US Navy

armed with a nuclear depth charge. If he found a target, he was to call the operations centre for orders whether to drop the weapon. If he could not contact the centre, then he was to call a backup location. In the event he could not reach either one, he was to "use his best judgement." Fortunately, he never had to make such a decision.

The first contact occurred on October 25, when the aircraft carrier USS *Essex* and destroyer USS *Gearing* tried to stop the tanker *Bucharest*. The tanker's captain refused, but the ship was allowed to proceed as it appeared to carry no military equipment. The next day the destroyer USS *Joseph P. Kennedy Jr.*, named for the President's late brother, stopped the Lebanese freighter *Marucla*. After an inspection it too was allowed to proceed.

As negotiation continued, the search continued for approaching ships, including the Soviet freighter *Grozny*, believed to be carrying fuel for the missiles. By October 26, four Soviet Foxtrot-class submarines were known to be operating in the area, two of them within the quarantine zone. These submarines were tracked by USN carriers and destroyers, a job made somewhat easier because they had to surface once a day to recharge their batteries.

On October 27, the Soviet submarine *B-59* sailed 100 miles south of Bermuda, on the northern edge of the quarantine zone. For two days the carrier USS *Randolph* tracked the submarine with its aircraft; the Soviet captain, Valentin Savitsky, kept *B-59* submerged that entire time, but now the batteries were running low and they had been unable to get new orders from Moscow.

Previously, the US had informed the Soviets that if a submarine were detected, the USN would drop practice depth charges, a weak explosive the size of a hand grenade, to signal the submarine to surface for questioning. However, this information had not been passed on to the local Soviet commanders.

With its ventilation system now broken, *B-59* surfaced and was quickly spotted by a Grumman S-2F tracker from *Randolph*. Savitsky ordered a crash dive before contact with Moscow could be made. The destroyer USS *Beale* arrived and dropped five practice depth charges on the submarine, then five more, receiving no response either time. Savitsky feared he was under attack and decided to fire one of the nuclear-tipped torpedoes the submarine carried, something allowed under his rules of engagement.

However, firing the torpedo required the assent of the three senior officers aboard; in this case the trio comprised Savitsky, flotilla commander Vasily Arkhipov and political officer Ivan Semonovich. Arkhipov vetoed the order, possibly averting nuclear war. *B-59* eventually surfaced and had to run on the surface for two days to fully recharge its batteries. It was shadowed by US ships the entire time; the American sailors even tried to defuse the situation by sending over chocolate and Coca-Cola, but the shipment accidentally fell into the sea and the Soviets ignored all attempts at communication. Afterward *B-59* submerged and reversed course.

The submarine *B-130* suffered engine failure and had to be towed home, and only one of the submarines actually reached Cuba. The rest returned home to an unhappy reception. However, the crisis ended in a negotiated withdrawal of the missiles from Cuba (along with a secret withdrawal of the American weapons in Turkey) and the standoff ended without nuclear Armageddon.

BELOW: The Soviet freighter *Bratsk* departs Cuba for the Soviet Union, carrying two missiles on its aft deck, November 9, 1962. Though the crisis had passed by that time, USN forces closely watched the withdrawal. US Navy

THE US NAVY IN VIETNAM

Air and sea power in Southeast Asia

Within a decade of France's failure to reconquer its former colony of Vietnam, the United States embarked on a campaign aimed at preventing democratic South Vietnam from being taken over by communist North Vietnam. It began with the employment of US advisors and military aid and soon expanded into full scale military operations involving hundreds of thousands of soldiers, sailors, marines and airmen. This included a massive commitment of United States Navy (USN) ships, aircraft and intelligence resources.

For their Vietnam operations, the USN took lessons from the French experience and its own past. The French Navy, especially its air arm, had performed well in Vietnam from 1946-54. Light carriers used leftover World War Two fighters and dive bombers to provide effective air support while French sailors and marines fought effectively along the coasts and rivers using surplus landing craft and local boats, all modified for sailing and fighting in rivers. The USN took notice of what the French did well.

Similarly, the USN had its own experience during World War Two and Korea of using carriers to strike targets on land, both at industrial and logistical targets and in close air support of troops in contact. These tactics came into use in Vietnam. It also used battleships, cruisers and destroyers to bombard targets along the coasts and engage enemy coastal shipping. The navy could still carry out amphibious operations along the coasts, landing Marines and transporting ground troops and equipment, a useful asset. While the roads were vulnerable to communist ambush and interdiction, the coastal waters were not.

Much of Vietnam's commerce and transport takes places on its

BELOW: USS *Midway* underway off the coast of Vietnam, April 1971. A Knox-class frigate is in the background, acting as escort. US Navy

numerous rivers and in the Mekong Delta. USN amphibious ships and craft, patrol boats and small ships, generally called 'riverine forces', worked to interdict communist efforts to deliver weapons and supplies using local craft such as junks and sampans, which blended effectively with the thousands of legitimate fishing and transport craft which ply the waters of the region. In this effort the USN looked back at its gunboat operations on the Mississippi River during the American Civil War.

American involvement in Vietnam expanded considerably after the Tonkin Gulf Incident in August 1964. North Vietnamese torpedo boats approached and subsequently attacked the American destroyer *Maddox*, which was on an intelligence-gathering mission off the coast. The US considered the attack unprovoked, not knowing the North Vietnamese thought the ship was involved in covert landing operations. A second US destroyer arrived and two days later they reported a second attack in rough weather. There is doubt as to whether the second attack actually occurred. One of the destroyers later reported there may have been misidentifications due to the weather and crew mistakes. Whatever the case, the incident led to a larger US presence in Vietnam and a widening of the war.

ABOVE: A North Vietnamese gunboat burns on the Roanay River after being attacked by aircraft from USS *Midway*, 1965. The shadow of an F-8 Crusader is visible on the water. US Navy

The USN's efforts during the Vietnam conflict can be simplified into four major areas, each of them pitting the USN's strengths, innovation and determination against that of the Viet Cong and North Vietnam.

The Air War: Air power is an American strength and was used to great effect in Vietnam. USN aircraft carriers played a major role in the various air campaigns carried out against North Vietnam. The carrier in particular was fairly safe from enemy attack, as North Vietnam lacked the naval capability to attack a carrier task force, and their air forces failed in the few attempts they made to attack USN forces at sea. It was far easier for them to make guerrilla attacks on air bases on land or ships in port.

Grouped into Task Force 77 (TF77) of the US 7th Fleet, US carriers operated freely off the coast, joining the first dedicated American air campaign, Operation Rolling Thunder, which began on March 2, 1965. The operation began two weeks late largely due to bad weather over North Vietnam; poor weather proved almost as great a foe as the North Vietnamese during the war.

The first navy strike occurred on March 15 with 94 aircraft from the carriers *Ranger* and *Hancock* bombing an ammunition depot at Phu Qui. Eight F-8 Crusader fighters arrived first, strafing the North Vietnamese air defences with cannon and rocket fire. The attacking force of 64 A-4 Skyhawks and A-1 Skyraiders struck the depot with general-purpose bombs, rockets, napalm and cannon fire. A Combat Air Patrol (CAP) »

LEFT: A swift boat fires its 81mm mortar at Viet Cong positions on the shoreline of the Gulf of Thailand, March 1968. US Navy

of 20 F-4 Phantoms, Crusaders and Skyraiders flew overhead to defend against opposing fighters, which never appeared. Five Skyraiders took damage from ground fire and one of them had to ditch in the ocean. A Search and Rescue (SAR) helicopter soon appeared overhead, but the pilot never exited his plane. After the raid two RF-8 Crusader reconnaissance aircraft photographed the extensive damage at the depot.

Such large attacks using aircraft from multiple carriers became known as 'Alpha Strikes', a term still used by the USN today to denote large air attacks. This initial attack set the standard for attacks carried out during the rest of the war. Tanker and electronic warfare aircraft also took part in such strikes when needed.

TF77 typically possessed three or four carriers with escorts. These carriers worked from two offshore areas. Yankee Station, sat southwest of China's Hainan Island and later moved farther north to better enable strikes against North Vietnam. Dixie Station sat 70 nautical miles (130km) southeast of Cam Ranh Bay, allowing carrier aircraft to range South Vietnam for close air support against Viet Cong and North Vietnamese Army (NVA) forces. TF77 generally posted two carriers at Yankee Station and one at Dixie Station. The fourth carrier would be in Subic Bay, Philippines for maintenance and crew rest, allowing the task force to rotate ships.

In mid-1965 the Navy assigned a fifth carrier to the region and by August 1966, enough airfields were completed for land-based tactical aircraft to allow Dixie Station to be shut down. Afterward all carriers operated at Yankee Station, although they could be called on to fly missions to the south at need.

TF77 stayed in constant action thanks to the efforts of the USN's Mobile Logistics Support Force, Task Force 73. These support ships carried out Underway Replenishments (UNREPs), delivering "beans, bullets and black oil." During Vietnam, the practice of 'vertical replenishment', using helicopters to transfer supplies between ships, began as well. The navy also introduced the Fast Combat Support Ship, an auxiliary which carried fuel, ammunition and refrigerated stores, providing everything a carrier task force needed aboard one vessel. These ships were designed to keep up with the task force as well.

As the air war continued, new tactics and weapons appeared, such as anti-radiation missiles to target the radars used to control surface to air missiles. North Vietnamese MiGs proved the need for American pilots to learn dogfighting and for modern fighters like the F-4 to be equipped with cannon in addition to their missile load.

US Navy pilots quickly adapted to the new threats of surface to air

ABOVE: Two PBRs patrol the Long Tau River, December 1966. The boats surface search radar and three .50 calibre machine guns made it a deadly threat to Viet Cong boat crews. NARA

LEFT: The battleship USS *New Jersey* fires a 16in shell at a target off the coast of South Vietnam, March 1969. US Navy

RIGHT: Multiple 20mm shells strike the water around North Vietnamese barges under attack by an A-4 Skyhawk from USS *Ranger*, July 1966. Interdicting supply shipments was a primary mission for the US Navy in Vietnam (US Navy

RIGHT: The destroyer USS *Orleck* fires its 5in guns at a Viet Cong position near Vung tau, March 1966. US Navy

BELOW: A Grumman A-6 Intruder from USS *Constellation* drops Mk 82 500lb bombs during a mission over South Vietnam in November 1968. US Navy

missiles and MiGs. One flight of four A-1 Skyraiders came under attack from a pair of MiG-17 jets. Far too slow to dogfight the newer, superior jets, the Skyraiders began flying one behind the other in a circle, where each could cover the aircraft ahead of it. When a MiG approached one Skyraider, the one behind opened fire on it with 20mm cannon. After the Americans shot down one MiG this way, the other disengaged.

Naval aircraft also dropped mines into and around North Vietnamese harbours, rivers and roads. Initially successful, the North Vietnamese soon found ways to avoid them. In March 1967, an A-4 Skyhawk from USS *Bon Homme Richard* successfully used the Walleye television guided bomb for the first time, flying the bomb through the window of a barracks.

Such weapons proved useful as the air war intensified from 1967. Targets previously considered off limits by political leaders were cleared for attack, including energy production and industrial sites. During the Tet Offensive in 1968, carrier aircraft flew over 3.000 sorties against North Vietnamese forces surrounding the US Marine outpost at Khe Sanh. The USN continued its air campaign throughout the war, winding down slowly as US forces withdrew and turned over responsibility to the South Vietnamese military.

In 1972 a North Vietnamese invasion threatened to overrun the South, »

RIGHT: The Douglas A-4 Skyhawk was a workhorse aircraft for the USN in Vietnam. This plane carries Mk 82 500lb bombs and AGM-12 Bullpup missiles during mission in November 1967. US Navy

prompting the US President, Richard Nixon, to authorise Operation Linebacker, a large-scale attack on North Vietnam. Up to six carriers at a time occupied Yankee Station for the operation. New precision munitions, such as laser guided and electro-optically guided bombs, saw wide use, downing bridges and smashing industrial infrastructure.

The Coastal War: While the carriers and their escorts stayed safely out to sea, USN cruisers, destroyers and frigates attacked the North Vietnamese coastline during Operation Sea Dragon. Using their 5in, 6in and 8in cannon, each destroyer was the equivalent of an artillery battery while each cruiser rivalled the firepower of an army artillery battalion. This duty was known as being on the gunline.

Their targets were coastal roads and railroad lines, coastal artillery installations and radar sites. Skyraiders and S-2 Tracker antisubmarine aircraft acted as spotters for the ships, which often operated in pairs. Over time, dozens of USN cruisers and destroyers took part in these missions, along with four destroyers from the Australian Navy.

Lighter forces, patrol craft and destroyer escorts, had another mission to interdict coastal shipping, which the North Vietnamese employed to carry weapons and supplies south. This task could be difficult due to the number of vessels along the coasts and their ability to duck into inlets and rivers to avoid detection. The USN gradually got better at this task, forcing the North

BELOW: The aircraft carrier USS *Oriskany* en route to Vietnam, June 1967. There are A-4 Skyhawks, F-8 Crusaders, A-1 Skyraiders and an E-2 Hawkeye on her flight deck. US Navy

LEFT: An F-8E Crusader fighter from USS *Oriskany* escorts a Soviet Tu-95 bomber sometime between 1966 and 1968. The Tu-95's long range made it useful for observation missions over US Navy ships off the Vietnamese coast. US Navy

Vietnamese to shift the transport of supplies inland through routes such as the Ho Chi Minh Trail.

In 1968 the US Navy pulled the battleship USS *New Jersey* from mothballs and deployed it to the Vietnamese coast, where it quickly proved its worth. On October 29, 1968, the ship fired at a hilltop artillery position but after six rounds the observer called for the ship to cease fire. The artillery position had been destroyed, and the hill was now 20ft lower. *New Jersey* withdrew to California for a refit in March 1969, but its return to Vietnam was cancelled and the ship returned to mothballs. In 1981 the navy revealed the battleship was removed to help draw the North Vietnamese into peace negotiations. They considered *New Jersey* a great threat due to her firepower and demanded the ship's withdrawal as a precondition.

During the 1972 offensive, ships on the gunline caused heavy damage to North Vietnamese Army armoured units moving near the coast. The North Vietnamese Air Force attacked ships on the gunline several times but never succeeded. Their coastal batteries had more success. Though they never managed to sink an American ship, their gunfire damaged 19 vessels and inflicted dozens of casualties.

War on the Rivers and Canals: Vietnam's interior waterways are critical to the country's life and economy. Its deltas are home to vital food production areas. The USN established Task Force 116, the River Patrol Force, in December 1965. Later, the US Navy teamed with the US Army to form the Mobile Riverine Force (MRF), which used river borne infantry units to engage NVA units operating in the delta.

These forces used a variety of small craft able to navigate shallow rivers and canals. The Patrol Boat, River (PBR) came in two versions, each just over 30ft long. The Mark II could make 30kts and carried three .50 calibre and one 7.62mm machine guns and a 40mm grenade launcher along with the crew's small arms. It proved so effective the PBR gained the nickname "Proud-Brave-Reliable."

Other craft included the 50ft Patrol Boat, Fast, also known as the Swift Boat. In addition to machine guns and a grenade launcher, it carried an 81mm mortar fired via lanyard. As the French had, the USN modified landing craft into heavily armed river monitors, command boats and transports called armoured troop carriers. The Assault Support Patrol Boats (ASPB) carried heavy armament and minesweeping equipment.

TF116 received air support from HU-1B Iroquois helicopters of Helicopter Attack Light Squadron 3 (HAL-3), joined later by Light Attack Squadron 4 (VAL-4) using the OV-10 Bronco aircraft.

The USN had no tactical doctrine for riverine operations, so the unit had to develop it. Rules were created for stopping and searching civilian craft while tactics covered operations using two boats operating in support of each other. Intense firefights could happen suddenly. In one successful engagement, a pair of PBRs with helicopter support destroyed dozens of Viet Cong sampans and junks after being ambushed on the Mekong Delta. The PBRs even rammed some of the enemy boats.

The MRF typically went after enemy units of battalion-size and larger. In addition to the armed monitors and patrol craft, it also used Army 105mm howitzers »

BELOW: The sturdy A-1 Skyraider could carry an impressive ordnance load and had a long loiter time, allowing it to remain over a combat area to provide support to ground troops. US Navy

LEFT: Carrier operations are inherently dangerous as fight decks are loaded with ordnance and fuel. The burning A-4 aboard USS *Forrestal* was struck by a rocket fired from a parked F-4, the accident caused by an electrical short and a missing rocket safety pin. US Navy

mounted on barges to fire barrages at enemy concentrations. An example of their operations came in January 1968 at Ben Tre, a city of 75,000. Eight hundred NVA troops attacked the city and soon pressed South Vietnamese troops and their US advisors into their small compound. Riverine forces poured gunfire into the NVA positions to pin them and resupplied the friendly forces. US troops soon retook the city.

As the war continued, riverine forces worked in-depth with Army troops and SEAL Special Forces troops on numerous operations to interdict enemy water movement and strike their units ashore. As the US began to withdraw from Vietnam in the early 1970s, South Vietnamese Navy forces began to assume full responsibility for riverine operations. Convoy operations also began to supply the Cambodian government with needed fuel and ammunition for its own part of the war.

The Intelligence War: While the role of carriers, aircraft and patrol boats is widely known, naval intelligence was a key player in Vietnam and the service gained experience which stood it well during the rest of the Cold War and beyond.

Photographic, signals and electronic intelligence were all collected and analysed. SEAL Teams carried out covert operations to emplace sensors and scout out enemy forces. Guided missile cruisers and destroyers used their powerful, long range search radars to study the skies over North Vietnam, analysing aerial activity and surface to air missile launches. Aerial reconnaissance aircraft did bomb damage assessments and photographed defences and facilities.

Naval aircraft were instrumental in determining that the Ho Chi Minh Trail served as North Vietnam's primary supply route for its forces in the south. Airborne intelligence squadrons flew missions so that specialists could monitor North Vietnamese radio transmissions. These missions often included Chinese and Russian interpreters

BELOW: The famous F-4 Phantom evolved into a tough, capable fighter-bomber in the skies over Vietnam. This F-4 from USS *Midway* drops Snakeye cluster bombs in 1965. US Navy

ABOVE: The nuclear-powered carrier USS *Enterprise* in the Tonkin Gulf in November 1972. From top to bottom her escorts, all nuclear-powered, are the cruiser *Long Beach* and destroyer leaders *Truxtun* and *Bainbridge*. US Navy

to listen in on the advisors helping supply North Vietnam and train its troops in some of the advanced weapons and equipment they provided. As the USN's air campaign grew during the war, these intelligence squadrons flew missions and learned to locate enemy air search and missile fire control radars, sometimes pinpointing them to within 50 metres.

Naval intelligence also reported on weapons smuggling by disguised North Vietnamese ships and boats. In one case the nuclear submarine USS *Sculpin* tracked a trawler as it left the Chinese island of Hainan with a load of weapons and ammunition. As it approached the Mekong Delta, South Vietnamese ships were summoned to stop the trawler. When the crew refused to heave to, the South Vietnamese ships opened fire. As *Sculpin's* captain watch through the periscope, the trawler took a hit which detonated its load of ammunition, blowing the ship to pieces.

The USN fought bravely and with great determination during Vietnam. However, no amount of courage could overcome the United States political establishment's lack of understanding of the determination of the North Vietnamese, or its own lack of will to seek a decisive end to the conflict. Like the rest of the American military, the USN used every resource at its disposal in a war it was not allowed to win.

RIGHT: A flamethrower equipped river monitor, nicknamed a 'Zippo Monitor', fires a stream of napalm at a target ashore in 1968. US Navy

INDO-PAKISTANI NAVAL WAR 1971

India and Pakistan challenge each other at sea

ABOVE: The Indian carrier *Vikrant* operating with a Sea King anti-submarine helicopter during the war. At this time, the Sea King operated from land, as *Vikrant* was not refitted to operate them until later. Indian Navy

Until 1971, Pakistan stood as a physically divided nation, with West Pakistan (now Pakistan) on India's northwest border and East Pakistan (now Bangladesh) sitting amidst India's eastern states. In March 1971, the Pakistani military moved to eliminate an independence movement in East Pakistan. Significant numbers of police and soldiers defected to the uprising, but by May the central government had regained control of most of the country. However, almost 10 million refugees had been driven into India and hundreds of thousands of citizens lay dead from the fighting. India supported independence for East Pakistan and gave support to the movement. Some fighting between Indian and Pakistani forces occurred and on December 3, 1971, Pakistan launched air strikes, starting a general war between the two nations.

The Indian Navy (IN) enjoyed a significant advantage over the Pakistani Navy (PN) in both numbers and types of surface warships. The IN possessed one aircraft carrier, two cruisers, five destroyers, 14 frigates, five anti-submarine corvettes, eight missile boats and four submarines. The PN fielded a cruiser, six destroyers, a frigate, and four patrol boats. Each navy also had various numbers of smaller craft such as minesweepers and support vessels.

Many of the combatant ships in both navies were former British Royal Navy types from World War Two. The IN also employed a number of Soviet-built missile boats and corvettes. The corvettes were not as seaworthy as the British-produced ships, but India's policy of non-alignment led it to acquire armaments from varied sources.

Pakistan kept most of its warships in West Pakistan, assigning the four patrol boats and some smaller craft to East Pakistan. The western city of Karachi housed the PN's major naval base. Once the war began the PN could not move ships from West to East Pakistan without a high risk of losing them. The PN sent one submarine, PNS *Ghazi* (the former USS *Diablo*) to the east, as it had a longer range than the PN's French-built Daphne-class units.

The Eastern Theatre

Ghazi set sail before the war began and was already in the Bay of Bengal. Its two missions were to sink India's carrier, INS *Vikrant*, and to mine the waters outside India's main eastern fleet base at Visakhapatnam. The submarine's crew spent ten days searching for the carrier to no avail before assuming its secondary mission. During the night of December 3-4 *Ghazi* began laying mines outside the harbour.

The Indian Navy knew *Ghazi* was in the area and dispatched the destroyer INS *Rajput* to sink the submarine. On the morning of December 4, *Ghazi* went down with all 92 of her crew, though the cause is still debated. The Pakistani Navy theorises that the submarine, while attacking *Rajput*, fired a faulty torpedo which circled and struck her, or else the hapless submersible hit one of its own mines. The Indian view is that *Rajput* sank *Ghazi* with depth charges.

The same day *Vikrant*, four escorts and three Landing Ship, Tank (LST) amphibious vessels approached the shore of East Pakistan hundreds of miles north. For the next two days *Vikrant's* small air wing attacked ports and shipping, sinking all four PN patrol boats, 11 merchant ships and destroying oil storage tanks at Chittagong. During December 7-8 *Vikrant's* planes knocked out the Pakistani Air Force's planes and airfields.

The *Vikrant* air wing included ten Hawker Sea Hawk fighters, armed with 20mm cannon, rockets and bombs. Four French-built Breguet Alize anti-submarine planes joined the fighters. These versatile turboprop aircraft could be armed as light bombers and proved very effective against small craft. The air wing took no losses during these operations.

Aware of the Indian landing force, on December 12 the Pakistanis mined the entrance to Chittagong Harbour, preventing a landing there. Instead, during December 14-15, the IN carried out a landing at Cox's Bazar, a small coastal city. *Vikrant's* air wing supported the landings, which were completed with difficulty, as the IN lacked experience in amphibious assaults. However, a reinforced battalion of Gurkhas came ashore unopposed. The successful landing cut of the possibility of Pakistani ground forces retreating into Burma.

The Western Theatre

As *Vikrant's* task force achieved success in the east, the IN enacted a plan to attack the main PN fleet anchorage at Karachi. The Indians believed the PN would keep its ships close to port to stay within combat range of their air force. When the war began four Indian missile boats (*Nipat*, *Nirghat*, *Veer* and *Vidyut*) were already positioned less than 200 miles from Karachi. Two anti-submarine corvettes, *Katchall* and *Kiltan*, along with oiler *Poshak* joined them. The corvettes had better radar and the oiler increased the missile boat's short operating »

BOTTOM: The Hawker Sea Hawk proved very capable against Pakistani ships and ground targets. This image shows a Dutch plane landing on a carrier in the 1960s. Dutch MoD

BELOW: A Breguet Alize takes off from INS *Vikrant* during the 1971 war. Designed for anti-submarine work, the versatile Alize could also carry rockets, bombs and even short-range missiles. Indian Navy

LEFT: INS *Vikrant* operating a decade after the war when the carrier was being fitted out to carry the Sea Harrier fighter. Five can be seen on the bow ahead of two Sea Hawks, four Sea King helicopters and four Alize anti-submarine planes. Arun Prakash

LEFT: The frigate *Khukri* was the only Indian warship sunk during the war, in a daring attack by the Pakistani submarine *Hangor*. Indian navy

range. All the missile boats were Soviet-built Osa-II class vessels, armed with four Styx anti-ship missiles and twin 30mm cannon.

On December 4, the entire task force began Operation Trident, moving to a point 200 miles south of Karachi, staying out of range of Pakistani air reconnaissance. After refuelling the task force moved toward Karachi, deploying with the missile boats in a diamond formation and the corvettes in the centre.

When the IN force was 70 miles from Karachi, the corvettes detected the PN destroyer *Khaibar* (ex-HMS *Cadiz*) 80 miles northwest. The missile boat *Nirghat* diverted toward *Khaibar* while the rest of the Indian ships maintained course for Karachi. Once within 20 miles, *Nirghat* fired a Styx missile. *Khaibar's* crew spotted it but thought they were under air attack and tried to engage the missile with gunfire. The missile struck the PN ship, which lost propulsion but remained afloat. Four minutes later *Nirghat* launched another Styx which also hit *Khaibar*. Within minutes the Pakistani ship sank, taking 220 of her crew to the bottom.

Ten minutes later, the Indian task force identified two more Pakistani ships. The destroyer *Shah Jahan* (previously-HMS *Charity*) escorted the merchant ship *Venus Challenger*, which carried a cargo of ammunition. INS *Nipat* fired two Styx missiles, one at each ship. One of them hit *Shah Jahan* in the stern, crippling the vessel, which was later towed back to Karachi. *Venus Challenger* took a hit amidships and quickly sank. The minesweeper PNS *Muhafiz* appeared a few minutes later from the northwest to investigate the explosions and INS *Veer* fired a single Styx which struck and sank *Muhafiz*. The minesweeper went down so quickly that the crew never had time to broadcast a radio report; 33 sailors died with their ship.

BELOW: PNS *Shah Jahan*, seen here as HMS *Charity* during the Korean War, had to be scrapped after the war due to the damage it suffered from a Styx missile. US Navy

RIGHT: Pakistan's air force played only a small part in the war at sea, although an F-104, at bottom left, did shoot down the Indian's Navy's only aerial loss, an Alize. Pakistani Air Force

Nipat continued on toward Karachi, taking a position 16 miles south of the harbour from where the crew fired their last two Styx missiles at the Kemari oil storage facility. One struck the complex, while the other crashed into the sea short of the target. At the same time, an Indian Air Force (IAF) raid arrived overhead, and the terminal suffered a number of hits which left it aflame. During this time, the Indian ships regrouped and returned south, with three sunk and one damaged Pakistani ships to their credit, along with damage done to the shore facilities.

The next day the Pakistani Air Force (PAF) sent two aircraft to attack the Indian missile boat's base at Okha. A B-57B Canberra bomber, escorted by one F-104 Starfighter, managed to destroy the jetty used by the missile boats along with much of their fuel and munitions. However. the missile boats themselves were not present, having been moved south in anticipation of just such an attack. On the way back from the raid the PAF F-104 found an Indian Alize on anti-submarine patrol and shot it down.

The heavy losses sustained in this attack caused the Pakistani command to organise civilian aircraft to fly volunteer reconnaissance missions. Naval officers frequently went on these flights and on December 6, one such flight, with naval observers aboard, incorrectly identified the PNS *Zulfiqar* (formerly the Royal Navy vessel HMS *Deveron*) as an Indian missile boat. Two Pakistani fighters strafed the ship before realising the misidentification.

The IN decided to attack Karachi again a few nights later. Operation Python began on the night of December 8-9 and the missile boat *Vinash* accompanied the frigates *Talwar* and *Trishul*, both UK-built Whitby-class frigates purchased by India. The frigates had better radar and communications suites than the missile boat. »

BELOW: A Daphne-class submarine of the Pakistani Navy underway after the war. The *Hangor* made the Pakistani Navy's only naval victory of the war when it sank the frigate *Khukri*. US Navy

ABOVE: India's submarines, such as this Soviet-built Foxtrot-class submarine, blockaded the Pakistani coast during the war. Indian navy

As the Indian ships approached Karachi, they were detected by a Pakistani patrol boat. *Talwar* sank it with her 4.5in and 40mm Bofors cannon. Meanwhile *Trishul* determined a Pakistani radar station had detected the Indian force. Despite the loss of surprise, the three ships continued toward Karachi. By 23:15 they reached a point 12 miles from the port and had detected several ships nearby.

Meeting no resistance, *Vinash* launched all four of its Styx missiles, three at nearby ships and one at the oil facility, which was still partially operational. The plan called for the missiles to launch in coordination with another air attack, but the ship launched early. All four missiles struck targets, one setting the oil terminal ablaze again. The three ships hit were two merchant ships, the Panamanian *Gulf Star* and British *Harmattan*, both sunk, and the PN oiler *Dacca*, heavily damaged. A few minutes later the air attack arrived overhead and the trio of Indian warships slipped away in the confusion.

As this attack occurred, three other Indian warships, the cruiser *Mysore* (ex-HMS *Nigeria*), destroyer *Ranjit* (ex-HMS *Redoubt*) and frigate *Betwa* (a Leopard-class built for India) steamed toward the Pakistani coast northwest of Karachi, assigned to attack coastal facilities and any ships in the area. While still well out to sea, they encountered a merchant ship which fled and began broadcasting a report of the Indian ship's presence and location. *Ranjit* put a shot across the merchantman's bow; it stopped and ran up a white flag.

It turned out the merchant ship was the Pakistani *Madhumati*. Its transmission was heard, as soon Pakistani aircraft arrived, circling overhead just out of range of the Indian group's anti-aircraft guns. Unwilling to risk losing ships, the Indian Navy command ordered a return to base; *Madhumati* came along as a prize, a reasonable return for a round or two of ammunition expended across its bow.

RIGHT: India used its Osa-class missile boats to great effect during the war, sinking six ships and damaging two more. US Navy

LEFT: The Pakistani frigate *Zulfiqar* was fired on by its own side, an all-too-common occurrence during the chaos of war. IWM FL2960

On the evening of December 9, the IN's 14th Frigate Squadron cruised 35 miles southwest of the Indian coastal village of Diu. A submarine contact had been detected in the area two days earlier. This was the Pakistani Daphne-class submarine *Hangor*, which fired a torpedo on the Indian frigate *Kirpan*. The crew detected the torpedo and turned away from it while firing anti-submarine mortars at the suspected location of their adversary. The torpedo missed or malfunctioned and *Hangor* set up another shot.

Another Indian frigate, *Khukri*, arrived in the area to assist and *Hangor's* crew fired their next salvo at the newcomer. The torpedo struck the frigate's fuel bunkers, sinking it in two minutes with a loss of 211 Indian sailors. *Kirpan* attacked with depth charges, but *Hangor's* crew fired another torpedo which struck the frigate in the stern, crippling it. *Hangor* escaped the area while *Kirpan* had to be towed back to port.

The war ended on December 16 with the surrender of Pakistani forces in East Pakistan. The conflict lasted 13 days, with the naval portion of the war a clear victory for the Indians. Pakistan suffered heavy losses including two destroyers, a submarine, a minesweeper, and ten patrol boats. Over 20 Pakistani auxiliary and merchant ships also fell to the Indian Navy, in addition to several vessels damaged and extensive damage to shore facilities such as the oil depot and naval bases. The Pakistani Navy suffered 1,900 dead and 1,400 taken prisoner. India's losses were far less at one frigate and one Alize aircraft lost, along with 214 dead naval personnel.

India's victory at sea in 1971 can be attributed to its larger and more advanced naval forces, which used carrier aviation and missile boats to make decisive and aggressive strikes against their Pakistani opponents. This quickly forced the PN into a defensive stance from which it did not recover before the war ended.

BELOW: The Pakistani submarine *Ghazi* began life as the USS *Diablo*. The sub was lost with all hands early in the war. US Navy

ISRAELI MISSILE BOATS IN THE YOM KIPPUR WAR

Innovation leads to victory at sea

ABOVE: An Osa class missile boat firing a *Styx* missile. At night in calm water, such a launch signature would be visible from many miles away. Public Domain

In the late afternoon of October 21, 1967, the Israeli destroyer *Eilat* was cruising along the Sinai coast near Egypt's Port Said. Lookouts spotted two missiles streaking toward the ship from the direction of the port. *Eilat's* captain ordered evasive manoeuvres but both missiles hit, causing casualties and heavy damage. The destroyer seemed recoverable until two more missiles launched an hour later. One struck *Eilat* and minutes later she sank. The deadly weapons were Soviet *Styx* anti-ship missiles, fitted on Egyptian patrol boats sitting within Port Said's harbour. *Eilat* was the first ship sunk by a missile boat during wartime, an ignominious fate and one which set the Israelis on course to a revived fighting navy.

The loss of *Eilat* was a severe blow to Israel's fledgling sea arm but it gave new impetus to a problem it had been working on since 1960. That year, a meeting took place to discuss how the navy might develop an edge despite its small budget and motley collection of aging second-rate warships. The defence minister told the facilitator of the meeting, Admiral Yohai Bin-Yun, no funding was available for new ships. If they could not improve using current resources, the navy would be reduced to a coastal defence force and the air force would assume its warfighting role.

One novel idea arose. Rafael, the Israeli government's weapons research arm, was working on a guided missile, the Luz, which had been rejected by both the army and air force. The missile packed a substantial 331lb warhead. If it could be fitted to a small craft, the navy would have a way to hit the Egyptians and Syrians. Admiral Bin-Nun decided the concept had merit and assigned Captain Shlomo Erell to determine if it could be done. Erell was a World War Two veteran of the British merchant marine and had survived two sinkings by torpedo during the war. He was determined to develop the idea, but he needed a working missile and a suitable boat design.

The Luz missile failed repeatedly during early sea trials. It was guided in flight by a controller using a joystick and binoculars, but this wouldn't work over the water; haze and humidity prevented the operator from tracking the weapon. During testing, a Rafael engineer, Ori Even-Tov, told a navy officer the missile needed a radar guidance system to track to the target, along with an altimeter to maintain a correct height above the waves. Erell heard about Even-Tov's idea and convinced him to take a job at Israel Military Industries (IAI), another company working on the missile project. Once at IAI, Even-Tov acquired textbooks on applicable theories and technology and got to work.

As he toiled, the threat grew. In 1962 the Soviet Union began providing missile boats to Egypt and Syria, increasing their ability to sink the freighters which were vital to Israeli national survival. Admiral Bin-Nun went to his superiors and warned them of the threat these missile boats posed. He also told them they had found a suitable boat design to carry the Luz once it was

ABOVE: The Soviet-designed Osa I missile boat served in both the Syrian and Egyptian navies. Three Egyptian and one Syrian Osa Is were lost to Israeli missiles during the 1973 war. US Navy

RIGHT: A *Styx* missile after removal from a former East German missile boat. *Styx* is the NATO reporting name for the missile; the Soviet name was the P-15 Termit,' or 'Termite.' (US Navy

ready. The Germans had a torpedo boat called the Jaguar, a development of their World War Two-era S-Boat. Bin-Nun received assurances the funding would be available once the missile was ready.

By 1964 Even-Tov's new missile design was in testing, but the missile would race into the air before diving straight into the ground. Three months later a second test had the same result. The engineer asked for nine months to fix the system. The next day a new employee, Yakov Becker, approached Even-Tov in his office. Yakov Becker had only a vocational school education, but he was sharp. He suggested the problem lay with the altimeter not being strong enough to withstand the pressures of launching. Even-Tov told Becker to fix the issue and Becker came back a few days later. When the project's two senior engineers both threatened to quit rather than try out Becker's idea, Even-Tov fired them and placed Becker in charge. Soon the missile had a new name – the Gabriel.

Months later, now 1965, the third test took place on a beach south of the port of Haifa. Many of the observers seemed convinced the weapon would fail. It seemed their prediction was true when the first missile crashed soon after launch. The second missile flew into the air, levelled off, and flashed out to sea. The observers began to cheer as the third missile was prepared. That weapon flew straight and true, striking the target to another round of cheers.

With the Gabriel nearly ready, others prepared the craft that would carry it. The Israelis had settled on the German Jaguar torpedo boat as the best option available in 1962. Years earlier Germany had pledged $60m in military aid to Israel; and part of that package was now a half-dozen Jaguars. In March 1963, Erell went to Germany with an Israeli naval architect to discuss modifying the boats. They wanted the design slightly enlarged to hold all the required equipment. After meeting with the builder, Lurssen Brothers, the local designers agreed it could be done.

However, by 1965, an Arab government heard of the deal and threatened to break ties with »

RIGHT: An Israeli Saar class boat and an Egyptian Osa class boat sailing alongside each other in 1979, after the two nations signed a peace treaty during the Camp David Accords a year earlier. Clandestine Immigration and Naval Museum

Germany if they built the boats for Israel. Instead, the Germans offered to pay to have the boats built elsewhere. Erell discovered by chance that Lurssen Brothers was working with a French company in Cherbourg to build patrol boats. The French firm agreed to build the boats there and began construction that year. The first was soon completed and subjected to over 10,000 miles of testing off the Normandy coast.

In Israel, Erell succeeded the retiring Admiral Bin-Nun and his technicians worked out the best way to outfit the boats as missile craft once they arrived. Fire control and radar systems had to be developed and all of it had to be allocated space in the increasingly cramped hull. Erell convinced his government to increase the total number of boats to 12, enabling the navy to fight Egypt and Syria simultaneously.

A major problem arose in 1967. The Six-Day War ended in Israeli victory, but shortly afterward *Eilat* was sunk, creating a crisis for Israel. The *Styx* missile had shown its capabilities, heretofore unrealised by Western militaries. Even worse, the *Styx* had a maximum range of 27 miles versus the Gabriel's 12. Any Israeli boat had to penetrate a 15-mile engagement gap where they could not respond to incoming fire. An Israeli electronics expert developed countermeasures, but until the navy faced the *Styx* in combat, there was no way to know if it would work. By 1969 five boats were delivered to Israel before yet another obstacle arose.

In late 1969 the French government decided to impose an embargo on deliveries of further craft. Patrol boats six and seven managed to get out of Cherbourg harbour just ahead of the embargo's imposition. The last five boats, already paid for, were complete but undeliverable. Someone proposed the boats should be crewed and snuck out of the harbour together. The Israeli government was reluctant to create

ABOVE: **A Gabriel missile launching for a Saar class missile boat. The missile had a smaller firing signature than the *Styx* but was smaller and had a shorter range.** Clandestine Immigration and Naval Museum

RIGHT: Two pre-refit Israeli Saar boats during a refuelling stop off the coast of Spain, December 1969. Clandestine Immigration and Naval Museum

RIGHT: A Saar 2 missile boat at speed. Note the five box launchers for Gabriel missiles and the 40mm Bofors gun turret forward. Clandestine Immigration and Naval Museum

BELOW: A line of Saar boats launches a salvo of Gabriel missiles in the mid-1980s. These boats were modernised versions of the ones which performed so well in 1973. Clandestine Immigration and Naval Museum

a serious incident with the French but nominally agreed the boats could leave, but only if it could be done 'not illegally', a noncommittal term which gave the Israelis on the scene freedom to act.

Those actions came quickly. In December 1969, the builders struck a deal to sell the five boats to a Norwegian ship-owner who wanted them to run supplies to North Sea oil rigs. It was a ruse. The Norwegian was a friend to the Israelis, providing the legal pretence for the boats to set sail. Still, concern arose that the French would see through the subterfuge and revoke their permission to depart so the Israelis decided to move quickly. Back in Israel an extensive logistics plan went into motion. Freighters diverted from their normal runs would set up refuelling rendezvous with the boats as they sailed the 3,200 miles to Israel. Since they could not enter any ports for fear of being impounded by local authorities, the boats would have to refuel at sea.

The commander of the flotilla, Captain Israel Kimche, decided they would depart on Christmas Eve, hoping the port authorities would be less alert. Unfortunately, a heavy gale blew in and nothing could leave the harbour. Then, at about 0200, the wind died down and the boats put to sea. Rocked by the heavy waters, they rendezvoused with the first refuelling ship, a freighter hiding in a cove on the Portuguese coast. The French soon discovered the ruse and elements of the government were so angry they demanded the French Air Force hunt the boats down. Fortunately, more moderate voices held sway, and the planes remained on the ground. The media jumped on the event, giving it widespread coverage.

Some reporters even rented planes to search the sea for the Israeli craft. A *Time* magazine article reported: "At various points, they were tracked by French reconnaissance planes, an RAF Canberra from Malta, Soviet tankers, the radar forests of the US Sixth Fleet, television cameramen and even Italian fishermen. From a distance, the world watched with emotions ranging from amusement to outrage." Finally, one media aircraft spotted the group navigating the Mediterranean, careful to avoid French waters. A second Israeli ship refuelled the boats near the southern tip of Italy, providing the fuel to reach Haifa on December 31, 1969. The risky yet bold plan paid off beautifully. »

LEFT: A *Styx* missile launches from a Komar class missile boat. This is an example in Polish service, but the Syrian and Egyptian navies used them., the Egyptians notably using them to sink the Israeli destroyer *Eilat* in 1967. Polish Archives

With all 12 boats now in Israel the navy fitted them out over the next three years. During this time, the boats received the class name Saar. Time for preparation ran out in 1973; during the first week of October all 12 boats took part in a fleet exercise. The day after they returned to port the various Arab nations attacked Israel, and the Yom Kippur War began.

With the pressure on, the flotilla's commanding officer, Captain Michael Barkai, quickly devised a plan. He had enough boats to face both Syria and Egypt, so six boats went south to guard against an Egyptian sortie while Barkai took five others north toward Syrian waters. The plan was to draw out the Syrian missile boats and sink them. The aggressive Barkai was so determined he told his men if the Syrians would not come out, they would go in after them with guns.

The Israelis did not have to wait long. A Syrian patrol boat was detected cruising 18 miles southwest of Latakia, Syria's primary port. The Israelis used their guns to disable the craft; one boat stayed behind to sink it while the rest continued toward Latakia. Within minutes they detected a Syrian minesweeper fleeing for port ahead. One eager captain fired a missile at maximum range, but the enemy vessel was out of range by the time the Gabriel arrived and it fell harmlessly into the sea. Another captain aboard a boat named *Reshef* let the range close another mile and fired. Two minutes later, the approximate flight time of the Gabriel, a large flash was seen on the horizon; the missile struck its target. A cheer went up on *Reshef's* bridge.

There was little time to rejoice as the Israeli radar picked up three new targets. Flashes on the horizon identified them as boats launching *Styx* missiles. Warning alarms sounded aboard the Israeli craft as the missiles raced toward them. Their crews activated electronic countermeasures and began evasive manoeuvres. As the boats turned and snaked through the waters their crews fired rockets overhead. Each burst flung strips of aluminium – chaff – into the air, sending confusing signals back to the Styx's radar. The countermeasures scrutinized those incoming radar waves and sent back more at the same wavelength, further confounding the enemy missiles.

As the Syrian missiles raced closer, tension mounted in the Israeli boats. Would the countermeasures work? As seconds ticked by, the situation shifted in the Israeli's favour. *Styx* missiles began to fall into the sea, fatally confused. None hit their target. There was exultation in the navy's war room back in Israel; they had been following the battle via radio. All their efforts had come to fruition. Their boats could both strike and defend.

Now the Saars advanced at their full speed of 40kts, rapidly closing the range gap. One Syrian boat changed course toward their opponents. The leading Israeli boat, *Gaash*, moved toward it. Before *Gaash* could get into range the Syrian fired a Styx. It was still in the air when *Gaash* reached 12 miles and fired a Gabriel.

BELOW: Tracers fly towards a *Styx* missile in flight, only its rocket exhaust visible, during a night battle. Effective countermeasures made the missile ineffective during the war. Yellow Apex via Wikimedia Commons

Moments later the *Styx* faltered, exploding as it hit the water. The Syrian boat launched another, but it exploded prematurely. Captain Barkai's boat, the *Miznak*, launched a Gabriel at another Syrian craft.

The Israeli missiles raced off toward the horizon and the crews soon saw flashes of light, followed by the rolling thunder of explosions. Both Syrian boats sank. The last Syrian warship, missiles expended, turn and ran for home. The Israelis gave chase. To save his crew the Syrian captain beached his boat along the coast, allowing the sailors to get ashore. Determined to finish the third ship, Barkai took his boat in to destroy it with cannon. Syrian shore batteries opened fire and shells began to fall around his boat, but Barkai continued, closing the range and wrecking the beached Syrian boat with gunfire. Returning to Haifa, the flotilla was greeted by crowds of proud citizens, cheering the sailors under the early morning sun. The flotilla sank five ships without loss and won the Battle of Latakia.

Just two nights later the Israelis took the fight to the Egyptians as well; it was time to avenge the *Eilat*. Six Saars sailed toward Alexandria. Soon radar detected four enemy craft. When the Egyptians reached their maximum range, they launched a salvo. The Israeli countermeasures again sent the enemy missiles crashing into the water. Undaunted, the Egyptian boats kept coming, launching another volley, then another. Missiles hurtled through the air; it would take only one to sink a Saar. However, none found a target that night. All of them fell into the sea.

The Egyptians were now 18 miles from the Israelis. Having shot their bolt, they turned toward home. Barkai ordered the flotilla to close to ten miles before firing to give them a chance to maximise hits. After a 25 minute stern chase one Israeli boat was in range. It fired a Gabriel which struck its target, just before another Saar fired and hit a second enemy warship. The Israelis fired again, hitting a third Egyptian craft which beached on the coast. The last enemy boat escaped when the Saar chasing it suffered engine problems, ending what is now known as the Battle of Baltim.

It was the last time Arab missile boats ventured out during the war. One would occasionally fire a *Styx* from the mouth of a harbour before ducking back to hide and a few would fire while hiding near foreign-flagged freighters, hoping to discourage return fire. The Saars tried to engage anyway, resulting in the loss of three freighters, including a Soviet ship. They also attacked oil tanks and port facilities. Their dominance of the battle area allowed Israeli cargo ships to reach Haifa with much-needed war materiel.

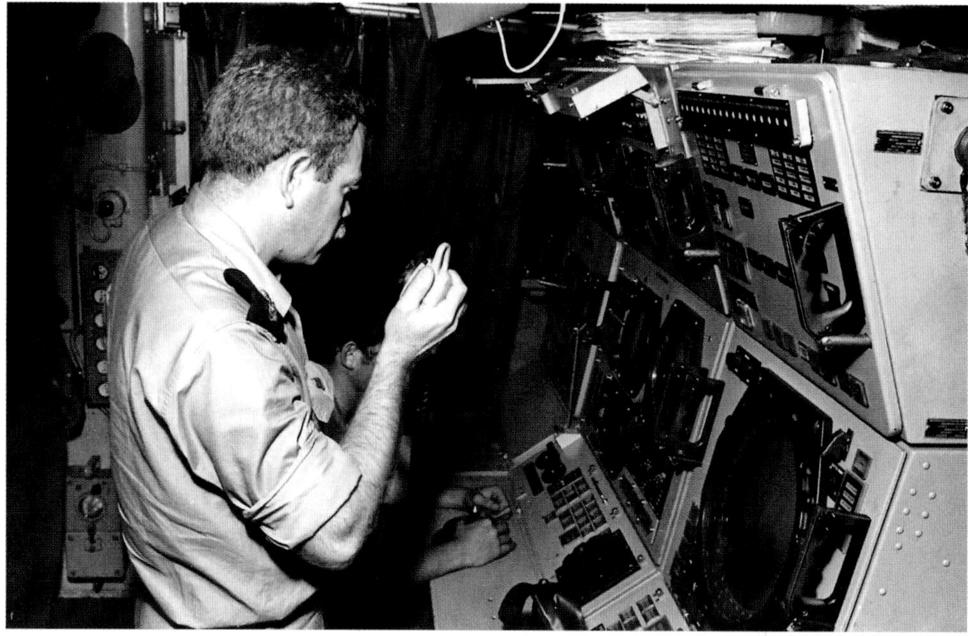

ABOVE: An Israeli officer monitors the control station for the Gabriel missile during a launch exercise shortly before the 1973 war. Yellow Apex via Wikimedia Commons

LEFT: A Saar boat (left) returns to dock the day after the Battle of Latakia. The crew quickly reloaded their expended munitions and prepared for their next mission. Yellow Apex via Wikimedia Commons

BATTLE OF THE PARACEL ISLANDS

China's first step into the South China Sea, 1974

RIGHT: The PLAN used two Soviet-built Project 122bis-type subchasers in the battle. This image shows a Polish ship of the same type. The PLAN used these ships for general patrol duties. Polish National Archives

On January 19, 1974, the navies of South Vietnam and the People's Republic of China fought a brief but intense battle in the waters around the Paracel Islands. A small battle fought with a small number of small ships; it nevertheless provided China with a victory it needed. At the Paracels China embarked on its slow, decades-long expansion into the South China Sea, an area it continues to claim and fight over today.

The islands are approximately equidistant from Hunan, China and Da Nang, Vietnam. Many nations laid claim to them during the 20th century, but by the early 1970s only South Vietnam and China seriously contended for them. Each side variously landed small groups on different islands, hoisting a flag or setting up a small base, only for the other side to respond and drive away their opponents. The Paracels do sit on the shipping lines from China to Singapore and ports south. The discovery of oil in the region only inflamed desires to possess the islands.

The opening moves occurred in October 1973 when two Chinese fishing vessels, Nos. *402* and *407*, set up a presence in the Paracel Islands. In November, South Vietnamese Navy (RVN) vessels arrived to chase the Chinese away. This back-and-forth struggle continued until January, when RVN ships rammed and fired warning shots at the Chinese vessels to drive them off. It was not the first time the Chinese had used militarised fishing vessels to enforce territorial claims and it's a tactic still in use today.

ORDER OF BATTLE

Ship	Armament	Type
Republic of Vietnam Navy (RVN)		
HQ-5	1 5in gun	Ex-USS *Castle Rock* (seaplane tender)
HQ-*16*		Ex-USS *Chincoteague* (seaplane tender)
HQ-*4*	2 3in guns	Ex-USS *Forster* (destroyer escort)
HQ-*10*	1 3in gun	Ex-USS *Serene* (minesweeper)
People's Liberation Army Navy (PLAN)		
No. *271*	1 85mm, 2 37mm cannon	Soviet Project 122bis-class submarine chaser
No. *274*	1 85mm, 2 37mm cannon	
No. *281*	4 57mm, 4 25mm cannon	Hainan-class submarine chaser
No. *282*	4 57mm, 4 25mm cannon	
No. *389*	2 37mm cannon	Type 010 ocean minesweeper, variant of Soviet Project 254 class.
No. *396*	2 37mm cannon	
Note: All ships also carried machine guns and small arms for crew use. Several ships had ground troops embarked.		

ABOVE: HQ-5 began life as the seaplane tender USS *Castle Rock*. This image shows the ship in 1944. US Navy

Four RVN ships, three frigates (HQ-*4*, HQ-*5* and HQ-*16*) and a minesweeper (HQ-*10*), remained in the area. All were formerly US Navy ships of World War Two vintage. Two of the frigates were former seaplane tenders and the third a converted destroyer escort, all transferred after service in the US Coast Guard. All had mechanical problems and were in disrepair, limiting their speed and performance.

The Chinese decided to respond with their own warships but had trouble assembling a task force. The Cultural Revolution had taken a toll on the People's Liberation Army Navy (PLAN) and its ability to keep ships in good repair. It managed to assemble a force of two submarine chasers, Nos *271* and *274*, along with two minesweepers, Nos *389* and *396*. Two other submarine chasers, Nos *281* and *282*, had to hastily sail 1,200km to get to the Paracel Islands and join the small fleet. The Chinese ships were all smaller than the RVN vessels.

The battle began on the morning of January 19, as the RVN ships approached the Chinese force in two groups, one from the south (HQ-*4* and -*5*) and another (HQ-*10* and -*16*) from the northwest. Both sides describe the subsequent fighting differently, making only general details available. The Chinese commanders were under orders not to start an incident and not to fire first, but if a fight began, they had to win. Subchasers *271* and *274* shadowed HQ-*4* and HQ-*5* while minesweepers *289* and *296* stayed with HQ-*10* and HQ-*16*.

HQ-*16* sent boats carrying Vietnamese commandos to two islands, both defended by Chinese militia landed earlier. Both Vietnamese groups were repulsed. During this time HQ-*16* rammed and damaged No *389*. The Vietnamese claim *389*'s crew fired small arms at them, which the Chinese deny. After this the RVN ships formed a battle line and attacked, opening fire. The initial RVN salvo hit the bridge of No *247*, killing its political officer and started a fire on No *389*, which took on water.

The Chinese version of events states the PLAN ships were now free to defend themselves, having been fired upon. As the PLAN ships were lighter and had shorter-ranged guns, their group commander ordered them to close the range, stating: "speed forward, fight close and hit hard." If the Chinese ships could get close enough, they would get under the guns of the larger RVN vessels and pound them with small calibre fire.

The tactic worked, with the range dropping from several kilometres to only a few hundred metres. The PLAN ships concentrated their fire on pilot houses, radars and communication antennae. Subchasers *271* and *274* focused on HQ-*4*, while minesweepers *389* and *396* pounded HQ-*16* with 37mm cannon shells. HQ-*16* soon withdrew with heavy damage. Switching their focus to HQ-*10*, the minesweeper hit the RVN ship's magazine, which exploded, and swept its decks with small arms, killing the captain. HQ-*16* attempted to help HQ-*10* but was driven back and retreated. After more firing, HQ-*4* and HQ-*5* withdrew as well.

The crippled HQ-*10* could not escape and when the *Nos 281* and *282* arrived, they finished the RVN ship with gunfire, sinking her. No *389* was also sinking but the fishing vessels, Nos *402* and *407* approached and pushed the minesweeper into shallow water, beaching her. The remaining RVN ships stood off to the south but did not engage.

It was a significant victory for the Chinese, who quickly reinforced with a frigate, five torpedo boats and eight patrol boats, carrying more infantry to put ashore. More ships were mobilised and the now outgunned Vietnamese realised they had lost and deescalated the situation. The victory is still celebrated in China, partly as it is one of few in the PLAN's relatively short history.

RIGHT: HQ-4 saw service with the US and South Vietnamese navies. Here, the ship cruises past Vietnamese boats in 1966. US Navy

MUTINY ON THE BALTIC

A zealous political officer takes over his ship

Mutinies are rare on a warship and practically unthinkable on any ship of the tightly controlled Soviet Navy. However, a revolt aboard a Soviet ship did occur in November 1975, and while few today know of the incident, it inspired a well-known novel and film in the following two decades.

The mutiny took place aboard the Krivak I-class frigate *Storozhevoy*. Designed primarily as an anti-submarine vessel using the SS-N-14 anti-submarine missile, the ship also carried surface to air missiles and two twin 76mm gun turrets along with torpedoes, giving it substantial combat capabilities. *Storozhevoy,* which translates as 'Sentry,' commissioned in December 1973 and was assigned to the Baltic Fleet.

LEFT: An Ilyushin Il-38 patrol plane flies over a Krivak I-type frigate in 1979. This type of aircraft proved crucial to locating *Storozhevoy* during her flight. US Navy

Captain Third Rank Valery Sablin instigated the mutiny. At the time he served as political officer ('zampolit') aboard *Storozhevoy*, with his primary duty being to maintain the Soviet political indoctrination of the crew. He was also fully qualified as an underway watch officer, a requirement on smaller ships like frigates. Unlike many political officers, Sablin became popular with the crew, showing concern for their problems. Over time, he managed to create a sense of personal loyalty to himself among many of them.

Sablin also developed a dissatisfaction with the ruling Soviet regime, believing its leaders were corrupt and had lost touch with the ideals of communism. He developed a plan to sail *Storozhevoy* from its moorings at Riga to the Kronstadt Naval Base in Leningrad (now St Petersburg). There he would start a popular uprising, enabling Soviet sailors and citizens to overthrow the existing government and create a true communist state. Whether a noble idealist or a man out of touch with reality, Sablin put his scheme into motion on the night of November 8, 1975, in the middle of the 58th annual celebration of the Russian Revolution.

He assembled the crew, though one third were away on liberty,

BELOW: The Krivak I frigate *Proyvisty* in 1987. *Storozhevoy* would have looked very similar to this ship. Note the twin 76mm gun turrets aft. US Navy

announced his plan and put it to a vote. Half elected to join him and those who declined were secured in their quarters. The ship's captain, lured below, was locked into one of the forward compartments. However, one of the officers who had voted for the mutiny managed to get off the ship and ran to report the situation. This forced Sablin to leave immediately, setting course through the Gulf of Riga at 30kts with lights out and the radar, detectable to other ships and aircraft, turned off. A sailor reportedly also managed to jump overboard, swim to shore and report the incident.

Despite these warnings, *Storozhevoy* got a two-hour head start, as the Soviet command did not believe the initial reports, thinking it a prank by drunken sailors. They were convinced when another officer aboard *Storozhevoy* managed to get free and send a radio message on an emergency frequency: "Mutiny aboard *Storozhevoy*. We are heading for open sea." Sent in clear speech, the message was picked up by the Swedish military.

Now spurred to action and believing the mutineers were defecting to Sweden, the Baltic Fleet scrambled aircraft and ships to search for the *Storozhevoy*. This included Il-38 patrol aircraft along with Tu-16 and Yak-28 bombers. On the waters of the Gulf of Riga, destroyers and patrol craft hurriedly set sail. All had orders to find the mutinous ship but fog and heavy local shipping traffic made the *Storozhevoy* hard to find. Radio traffic intercepted by the Swedes contained orders to stop and return to port, including promises of pardons if the mutineers returned.

As *Storozhevoy* passed from the Gulf of Riga into the Baltic, lighthouse tenders spotted her, allowing the search planes to narrow their focus. The critical point came when *Storozhevoy*'s crew, for unknown reasons, turned on their radars. The combat aircraft closed in, ordered to attack the ship. The Swedes later reported "very stormy conversations" between the bomber crews and ground control, as the pilots did not want to fire on Soviet sailors. One aircraft refused to fire at all and returned to base. The rest dropped bombs near the ship and some fighters fired shots across the bow, but *Storozhevoy* kept sailing with no response and no return fire.

Eventually, direct attacks began, although reportedly one of the pursuing ships, also a Krivak I frigate, was struck by accident. *Storozhevoy* took cannon fire and bomb hits, jamming its rudder and flooding the stern. When two missile boats got within range, it was clear the mutiny had failed. Some sailors released the captain, who shot and wounded Sablin. At 10:30, the captain signalled he had regained control of the ship, which stopped east of the Swedish island of Gotland.

The Soviets tried to cover up the incident by running an exercise the next day and reporting an accidental firing incident. The Baltic Fleet painted *Storozhevoy's* hull number on another Krivak I frigate and sailed it around the Baltic. The entire crew was detained, with the main conspirators being charged. The other officers, including the captain were all demoted one rank. Sablin received a quick trial and execution. A US naval officer wrote a largely accurate thesis about the incident in 1982. An aspiring author named Tom Clancy read this paper and used it as a basis for his bestselling book *The Hunt for Red October*, which later also became a film.

ABOVE: A Yak-28 bomber in flight. It appears the only time a Yak-28 engaged in combat was against the *Storozhevoy*. USAF

LEFT: The Krivak I frigate *Zharkiy* launches smoke canisters during an exercise. Their use would have provided only a temporary reprieve from Soviet aircraft during *Storozhevoy*'s brief mutiny. US Navy

THE TANKER WAR

Iran and Iraq's destabilising naval campaigns 1980–88

RIGHT: The Iranian minelayer *Iran Ajr* after boarding by the US Navy. Mines were found aboard the ship, which was then scuttled. US Navy

Long-simmering tensions between Iraq and its eastern neighbour Iran boiled over into war in 1980. Iraq's leader, Saddam Hussein, aspired to dominate the Persian Gulf region and take advantage of Iranian weakness in the aftermath of its revolution. The Iranian forces were desperately short of spare parts to operate their US and British-supplied weapons due to ongoing arms embargoes. Even worse, purges carried out by Iran's new revolutionary government had killed, jailed or exiled many of the nation's experienced officers, pilots and technicians. However, after initial Iraqi gains, the war stalemated due to Iranian resistance and Iraqi miscalculation.

As both nations had extensive sea trade, naval operations were inevitable and quickly commenced. Iran, though short of missiles and other modern ordnance, still had a professional core in its navy, which quickly forced the Iraqi Navy to remain in port. This also prevented Iraq from exporting oil using tankers. Meanwhile, the Iranians remained able to export oil and carry out commerce through shipping.

In May 1981, Iraq declared that all ships entering or departing from Iranian ports would be subject to attack. Initially the Iraqi regime focused on ships believed to be carrying military supplies but this policy was soon expanded to attacking ships carrying exports. For the next two years the Iraqis used Mirage F-1 and MiG-23 fighters along with French-built Super Frelon helicopters for shipping strikes. The Exocet missile became the preferred weapon for these attacks, and all three aircraft types could employ them. During this period, the Iranians generally refrained from attacking civilian shipping, focusing on the Iraqi Navy.

However, in 1984, Iraq began to operate the Super Etendard which had a longer range and also carried the Exocet. The Iraqis also used the aircraft against Iran's Kharg Island oil facility, important for that nation's economy. Iran began attacking Iraqi tankers, later expanding to ships of nations supporting Iraq or carrying its oil. As the Iranians lacked effective anti-ship missiles due to the embargo, they used anti-tank and land attack missiles such as the Maverick and AS-12. These attacks escalated and soon became known as the 'Tanker War'.

In actuality, oil tankers that were struck tended to absorb missile

BELOW: The frigate USS *Stark* lists heavily to port after being struck by a pair of Iraqi Exocet missiles, May 17, 1987. The circumstances of the attack are still unclear. US Navy

damage fairly well and relatively few were sunk. Overall oil shipments were hardly affected; even at its height, the Tanker War never disrupted more than 2% of ships transiting the Gulf. Though the fighting resulted in the death of 116 merchant sailors and drove up insurance rates, it had little other effect.

To remain fighting, the Iranians improvised. They employed small boats fitted with heavy machine guns and Rocket-Propelled Grenade (RPG) launchers to attack shipping. The Swedish Boghammer design was widely used by Iran, with the name becoming a nickname for any Iranian armed boat. They also used helicopters carrying anti-tank missiles and their dwindling supply of Mavericks. Iranian warships also boarded and fired upon civilian shipping.

In return, the Iraqi Air Force used fighters in 'buddy' teams to extend their range and attack previously unreachable Iranian bases and ports. One fighter carried ordnance while the other carried refuelling tanks to keep both planes in the air longer. Eventually the air attacks from both sides got bad enough that Kuwait requested the assistance of foreign powers to protect their ships. The Soviet Union did so first, chartering tankers and escorting them. US law prevented US Navy (USN) ships from escorting foreign ships but the United States eventually agreed to reflag 11 tankers as American ships so they could be protected.

This was known as Operation Earnest Will and brought the USN into a conflict growing increasingly dangerous and chaotic. On March 17, 1987 two Exocets from an Iraqi Mirage hit the frigate, USS *Stark*. The ship stayed afloat, but 37 sailors died. Iraq claimed it was an accident and apologised.

What eventually brought the situation to a crisis was the Iranian use of mines against civilian and naval vessels. The USN found the Iranian ship *Iran Ajr* laying mines, boarded it and found proof of the minelaying campaign. Afterward the ship was towed to international waters and scuttled.

Iran also acquired Chinese-made *Silkworm* anti-ship missiles, a version of the Soviet *Styx*. After two US-flagged tankers had been hit the USN shelled an Iranian oil platform, under Operation Nimble Archer. And, when a USN frigate struck a mine in April 1988, the incident led to Operation Praying Mantis (see page 72), which caused heavy losses to the Iranian Navy.

The final tragic event in this undeclared war came on July 3, 1988 when the cruiser USS *Vincennes* accidentally shot down an Iranian airliner carrying 290 passengers after it was misidentified as an attacking aircraft. Though the loss of life was terrible, the incident highlighted how bad the situation had become and caused a cooling of tensions. Iran and Iraq finally agreed to a ceasefire in August 1988.

ABOVE: An American F-14 Tomcat intercepts an Iranian P-3 Orion patrol plane over the Indian Ocean in 1981. The Orion is a versatile aircraft and can carry an assortment of anti-ship and anti-submarine weapons. US Navy

BELOW: An Iranian oil platform burns after an attack. The Iranians often based troops on such platforms to help coordinate actions in the Persian Gulf. US Navy

FALKLANDS CRISIS 1982

The naval campaign around the contested islands

ABOVE: A super Étendard strike aircraft of the Argentine Navy. Each could carry a single Exocet. Argentine Government

Argentina has long claimed the Falkland Islands, some 300 miles east of the Argentine coast. Known in that country as the Malvinas, the islands were (and are) remote, barren and subject to harsh weather conditions. However, by 1982 the Falklands had been a British possession for a century and a half. They served as a coaling station during World War One and while the islands seldom figured prominently in English policy, the inhabitants considered themselves British citizens.

During the 1960s and 70s, negotiations between the UK and Argentina about possession went on with little progress but by the early 1980s, Argentina's chances seemed to improve. British defence cuts reduced the defences of the Falklands, including the withdrawal of the Royal Navy ship, HMS *Endurance*, without replacement. Argentine leaders decided they could invade the islands using minimal force and present the UK with a fait accompli, which the British would have no choice but to accept.

At the time, Argentina had one of the best navies in South America, with an aircraft carrier and escorts, a light cruiser, submarines and smaller warships and support vessels. Two of their destroyers were British-built Type 42s, also used by the Royal Navy. The naval air arm possessed A-4Q Skyhawks and Super Etendards while the Argentine air force had bombers, fighters and strike aircraft (see table). Significantly, the Argentines possessed the French-made Exocet anti-ship missile, though they only had five of the air-launched variant.

The initial Argentine plan called for action later in 1982, but a situation on South Georgia Island, 800 miles southeast of the Falklands, accelerated their schedule. An Argentine scrap metal dealer landed on South Georgia without a permit from the British authorities, provoking a British response. The incident provided an excuse to launch the Falklands invasion, named Operation Rosario, on April 2, 1982.

Two Argentine ships, *Cabo San Antonio* and *Isla de los Estados*, carried a marine battalion including LVTP-7 amphibious armoured vehicles to capture Port Stanley,

the largest population centre. Their escorts consisted of the two Type 42 destroyers and two corvettes. An icebreaker with a helicopter carried marines and soldiers for landings at Goose Green and Darwin. The carrier *25 de Mayo* and three destroyers provided air cover and a submarine landed a reconnaissance party. After a short fight against the small force of Royal Marines stationed on the island, the Falklands were in Argentine hands.

Argentina also sent a force to capture South Georgia. Days earlier, HMS *Endurance* had dropped a section of 22 Royal Marines on the island but the vessel was under orders to stand clear and not engage opposing forces. The Argentine transport *Bahia Paraiso* and corvette *Guerrico* arrived at the settlement of Grytviken on April 3 and ordered the population to surrender via radio. Royal Marine Lt. Keith Mills tried to convince them to retire, but the Argentine ships commenced landing operations.

ABOVE: An Argentine Air Force A-4C Skyhawk parked at its airfield during the Falklands Crisis. Note the ship symbol painted below the canopy. US Navy

The marines engaged, hitting the *Guerrico* with a round from an anti-tank launcher, killing one crewman and wounding five. The corvette withdrew out of range and opened fire with its 100mm gun. The British marines also managed to shoot down one of the Argentine's two helicopters, causing two dead and two wounded. However, the Argentines continued to land, and soon the situation compelled the outnumbered British force to surrender. The marines were soon evacuated and repatriated, Mills receiving a Distinguished Service Cross for this actions.

However, rather than accepting the loss of the Falkland Islands, the British government under Prime Minister Margaret Thatcher, ordered a campaign to retake the islands. Negotiations commenced as well, though if those failed, the military operation would proceed. The Ministry of Defence quickly assembled a naval task force which left for the Falklands in stages. The first three vessels were the nuclear attack submarines *Spartan*, *Splendid* and *Conqueror*. Next, Rear Admiral John Woodward's First Flotilla of four destroyers and three frigates received orders redirecting them from the Mediterranean.

In the UK, the navy gathered ships which were in port returning from deployment, or about to leave. This included the two aircraft carriers *Hermes* and *Invincible* with 20 Sea Harrier fighters, five frigates and destroyers, the landing ship *Fearless* and a number of support vessels. To provide sufficient transport and logistics capabilities, dozens of civilian ships were temporarily taken into service, known as Ships Taken Up From Trade (STUFT). Including ships dispatched later, the full British combat force amounted to two carriers, eight destroyers, 15 frigates, and six submarines, plus amphibious ships, transports and auxiliaries, commanded by Rear Admiral Woodward. In addition, the liner *Queen Elizabeth II* was converted to a troopship for the conflict.

Ascension Island, 4,260 miles from Great Britain and 3,915 miles from the Falklands, became an effective halfway point for British naval forces. It served as a logistics hub and had a runway large enough to handle bombers and cargo aircraft. Years later, declassified US files revealed the US government »

LEFT: The destroyer HMS *Cardiff* anchored near Port Stanley after the war. The transport SS *Canberra* is in the background. Ken Griffiths

LEFT: The light cruiser *General Belgrano*. Though outdated by 1982, the ship's firepower and range could have been significant in a surface engagement. Argentine Government

diverted a supertanker to the island to provide fuel for the British forces transiting to the Falklands. The US Government also had a plan to 'loan' the UK an aircraft carrier, complete with 'technicians' to help operate it, in the event a British carrier was lost.

The first part of the British plan, Operation *Paraquet*, focused on recapturing South Georgia Island. A small force including *Antrim*, *Plymouth*, and *Endurance*, later joined by *Brilliant*, sailed to the island with 220 Marines and SAS troops around April 18. The weather proved brutal, hampering the landing of SAS on the island and causing the loss of two of the group's Wessex helicopters. The Argentine submarine *Santa Fe* operated in the area and even spotted *Endurance* recovering a Royal Marine's reconnaissance party, though its commander chose not to attack it.

On April 25, HMS *Antrim*'s helicopter spotted *Santa Fe* on the surface and attacked it with depth charges. The submarine suffered enough damage to prevent it from submerging, so it made for Grytvitken on South Georgia. More British helicopters arrived, strafing and hitting the submarine with AS-12 missiles, starting a fire and causing *Santa Fe* to list heavily. She managed to reach the dock but was crippled, taking no further part in the fighting. Having gained the initiative, the British task force quickly attacked the Argentine forces ashore, which soon surrendered, putting South Georgia back in British possession.

On April 29, the British War Cabinet announced a Total Exclusion Zone (TEZ) of 200nm around the Falklands. This meant that any ship or aircraft within the zone would be assumed to be hostile. Simultaneously, the submarine *Splendid* received orders to attack the Argentine carrier *25 de Mayo* without warning if it was found near the islands. The following day the British carrier group entered the TEZ.

Hours later a Vulcan bomber attacked Stanley Airport, dropping 21 1,000lb bombs. Several of these struck the runway, leaving large craters which the Argentines could not easily repair. Critically, this left the airport unable to operate Argentine strike aircraft. Raids by Sea Harriers caused further damage to Stanley Airport and the airfield at Goose Green.

Also on April 30, HMS *Glamorgan*, HMS *Alacrity* and HMS *Arrow* shelled Stanley Airport and in return were attacked by three Argentine Dagger aircraft, Israeli copies of the Mirage 5. Their bombs missed but they hit *Arrow* with cannon fire. A second attack by Daggers lost one aircraft to a Sidewinder fired by a Sea Harrier.

HMS Brilliant and HMS *Yarmouth*, hunting submarines to the north, weren't aware that the submarine *San Luis* found and attacked them, but its torpedo's guidance failed. The Argentines next dispatched

BELOW: Sea King helicopters pick up survivors of HMS *Coventry* from the water. The ship sank quickly, with 20 sailors killed in the attack. IWM FKD1274

six Canberra bombers to attack the ships in two groups of three. The first group did not attack, while the second was found by the Sea Harriers of a British Combat Air Patrol (CAP), losing one bomber to a Sidewinder. The CAP also engaged two Mirages, downing one with a missile. The other crashed while avoiding friendly fire from Stanley.

The Argentine carrier group hunted throughout April 30 for the British force; an S2 Tracker reconnaissance plane discovered the British that night but had to retreat when a Harrier was scrambled to intercept it. The fleeing Tracker led the Harrier straight back to the Argentine carrier and its escorting Type 42 destroyers, one of which locked onto the Harrier with the tracking radar of its Sea Dart missile system. Now both sides knew the location of the other but were unable to launch effective strikes due to the range and the limited number of Sea Harriers available to the British.

The British lacked an airborne reconnaissance and early warning capability, instead using their nuclear submarines to search for the enemy. On the morning of May 2, while the two carrier groups manoeuvred, the submarine HMS *Conqueror* trailed the Argentine cruiser *General Belgrano* and its escorts, which steamed south of the Falklands. Another small task force of missile-armed corvettes sailed north of the Argentine carrier. Argentine naval leadership hoped to catch the British task force in a form of pincer movement, with each group attacking in turn. The British put its own Type 42 destroyers forward as a picket line, with the remaining escorts protecting the carriers and auxiliaries.

ABOVE: Harriers lined up on the flight deck of HMS *Hermes*, May 19. The three aircraft with camouflage paint are GR3 ground attack variants. RAF Historical Branch

HMS *Conqueror* was in position to attack the *Belgrano* but she was outside the TEZ. However, it represented a grave threat with its 15 6in guns and *Conqueror* risked losing contact if the Argentine cruiser went over the Burdwood Bank, a shallow, jagged area of the sea bed where the submarine could not safely follow. The War Cabinet in London approved an attack due to the threat and circumstances.

The *Belgrano*'s crew had no idea they were being shadowed by a British submarine and were not at defensive stations. At 1,400 yards, the sub launched a trio of unguided torpedoes. Two hit the cruiser, one aft, killing many sailors in a mess deck area and knocking out electrical power, and the other forward, just ahead of the forward gun turret. The ship filled with smoke and took on water. Unable to save their ship, the crew abandoned her a half hour after the attack. Fifteen minutes later the *General Belgrano* sank. The escorts, one damaged by the third torpedo which failed to explode, gave chase but *Conqueror* escaped. When the Argentine ships returned to rescue survivors, they had been scattered by heavy seas. It took two days to recover them, with 321 sailors dying in the attack.

The Argentine Navy immediately recalled the rest of its ships, including the carrier group, to port. On May 3 helicopters from HMS *Coventry* and HMS *Glasgow* attacked the patrol ship *Alférez Sobral* using Sea Skua anti-ship missiles. The ship limped back to port while the *25 de Mayo* managed to evade *Splendid* over the next five days and return to Argentina as well.

However, on May 4, the Argentines showed the Royal Navy they were still prepared to fight. A pair of Super Êtendards, each carrying an Exocet »

RIGHT: A Chinook helicopter hovers over the aft deck of HMS *Bristol* during a supply delivery at Ascension Island.
Ken Griffiths

missile, attacked the British Type 42 destroyers, still on radar picket duty. As the Argentines also had Type 42s, they were aware its radar was most effective for detecting high-flying aircraft. The two pilots came in low, only 100 feet above the water. At 25 miles, they came up to 1,000 feet and launched their missiles. Detected by *Glasgow*, the aircraft turned for home while the Exocets raced toward *Glasgow* and *Sheffield*.

One missile hit HMS *Sheffield* amidships while the other went into the ocean east of the destroyers. Fires raged on *Sheffield*, which lost power and could not signal for help. A patrolling Sea King helicopter spotted the smoke plume and responded, relaying information to the task force. More helicopters and two frigates made for *Sheffield*, but the fires grew unmanageable as the ship lost water pressure to its hoses. The crew abandoned ship, with 20 dead and 24 wounded. The destroyer was taken under tow but sank in heavy seas on May 10.

Over the next several days three Harriers were lost, one to anti-aircraft fire during an attack on Goose Green and two likely collided in foggy weather. The Argentines repaired the airstrip at Stanley and began sending C-130 cargo aircraft to resupply the garrison but had trouble launching strike missions due to weather. Admiral Woodward's staff devised a plan to pair a Type 42 destroyer with a Type 22 frigate and attempt to lure enemy strike aircraft into attacks. The Type 42 would engage with its medium range

BELOW: RFA *Olna* refuelling ships of the task force en route to the Falklands. This image was taken from HMS *Cardiff*.
Ken Griffiths

Sea Dart missiles, while the Type 22 would protect the ships with its short-range Sea Wolf missiles. This combination was known as a '42/22' or a 'Type 64.' On May 9 *Coventry* fired on two Skyhawks escorting a C-130; both crashed, possibly colliding, while trying to avoid the missiles.

On May 7, the Argentine trawler *Narwhal*, in use as a spy vessel, took heavy damage from Sea Harriers. One crewman died and the rest were taken prisoner before the vessel sank. On May 11, frigate *Alacrity* found a transport attempting a supply run. The British ship opened fire, striking ammunition on the transport, which exploded. Soon after, the Argentine submarine *San Luis* fired a torpedo at *Alacrity* and sister ship *Arrow* but the weapon missed. The British ships were unaware of the attack at the time.

On May 12, the '42/22' was *Glasgow* and *Brilliant*. Attacked by four Skyhawks, the Sea Dart system on *Glasgow* failed to engage the aircraft and its 4.5in gun jammed after a shore bombardment mission. *Brilliant* fired its Sea Wolf system, destroying two Skyhawks and causing a third to crash while avoiding a third missile. The fourth plane withdrew but its windscreen was so encrusted with salt spray from the low altitude flying it crashed on landing. None of the aircraft scored any hits.

An hour later four more Skyhawks attacked, and this time both missile systems failed to function. One bomb struck *Glasgow*, passing through the ship without exploding but causing serious damage, nonetheless. One Skyhawk succumbed to friendly fire while returning home, but *Glasgow's* damage forced her return to England for repairs.

On May 18 helicopters from HMS *Hermes* carried SAS troops and a naval gunfire support team to Pebble Island, where they attacked an Argentine airstrip. They destroyed 11 aircraft, and HMS *Glamorgan* provided fire to cover their retreat. Three days later Sea Harriers bombed two Argentine cargo vessels near the islands. The crew abandoned one while the other was left dead in the water.

The Amphibious Group entered the TEZ on May 18 and began preparing for the landings. Several GR3 Harriers from the RAF were transferred to *Hermes*. These aircraft had better ground attack capabilities than the Sea Harriers. Two days later the landing group and its escorts set out for San Carlos to land four battalions of Marines and Paras. »

BELOW: The carrier HMS *Hermes* steams alongside HMS *Broadsword* in 1982. The ski-jump deck on the carrier allowed Harriers to take off with more fuel and weapons aboard. IWM MH27508

NAVAL COMBATANTS AND AIRCRAFT IN THE FALKLANDS CRISIS			
United Kingdom			
Type	Class	Armament	Ships
Aircraft Carriers	Invincible	Sea Dart, Sea Harriers, Sea Kings	*Invincible*
	Hermes	Sea Cat, Sea Harriers, GR3Harriers, Sea Kings	*Hermes*
Destroyers	Type 42	4.5in cannon, Sea Dart,	*Sheffield, Glasgow, Coventry, Cardiff, Exeter*
	Type 82	4.5in cannon, Sea Dart, Anti-sub mortar	*Bristol*
	County	4.5in cannon, Sea Slug, Sea Cat, Exocet	*Glamorgan, Antrim*
Frigates	Type 22	Sea Wolf, Exocet	*Broadsword, Brilliant*
	Type 21	4.5in cannon, Sea Cat	*Ambuscade, Antelope*
	Type 21	4.5in cannon, Sea Cat, Exocet	*Active, Alacrity, Ardent, Arrow, Avenger*
	Type 12	4.5in cannon, Sea Cat	*Plymouth, Yarmouth*
	Leander	Sea Cat (Sea Wolf in Andromeda), Exocet	*Andromeda, Argonaut, Minerva, Penelope*
Submarines	Diesel-Electric	6 21in torpedo tubes	*Onyx*
	Nuclear	5 or 6 21in torpedo tubes	*Conqueror, Courageous, Valiant, Splendid, Spartan*
Aircraft			
Type	Primary Role	Armament	
Sea Harrier	Air Defence, strike	30mm cannon, Sidewinder missiles, bombs, rockets	
GR3 Harrier	Ground attack	30mm cannon, Sidewinder missiles, bombs, rockets	
Vulcan	Bomber	21 1,000lb bombs	
Argentina			
Type	Class	Armament	Ships
Aircraft Carrier	25 De Mayo	SkyHawks, Trackers, Sea Kings	*25 De Mayo*
Cruiser	General Belgrano	15 6in, 8 5in cannon, Sea Cat	*General Belgrano*
Destroyers	Type 42	4.5in cannon, Sea Dart, Exocet	*Hercules, Santisima Trinidad*
	Sumner	5in cannon, Exocet	*Hipolito Bouchard, Piedra Buena, Segui*
	Gearing	5in cannon, Exocet	*Comodoro Py*
Corvettes	A69	3.9in cannon, Exocet	*Drummond, Granville, Guerrico*
Aircraft			
Type	Primary Role	Armament	
Mirage III	Fighter	*Magic* missiles	
Dagger	Strike	Bombs, *Shafrir* missile	
A-4B/C Skyhawk	Strike	Bombs	
Super Étendard	Strike	Exocet, Magic missiles	
A-4Q Skyhawk	Strike	Bombs, Sidewinder missile	
Pucara	Ground attack	Rockets, bombs	
Canberra	Bomber	8,000lb of bombs	

Notes: Magic and Shafrir are air to air missiles. British forces used the AIM-9L Sidewinder, with superior engagement capabilities

The escort of one destroyer and six frigates would have to protect the landing force against whatever the Argentines threw at them, until the landing force was solidly ashore.

Though not without difficulty and loss, the landings succeeded, setting up the ground force for advances on Gooses Green and Stanley. On May 21, HMS *Ardent* bombarded Goose Green from 20km distance and two Argentine Pucara light attack aircraft took off to search for the source of the incoming fire. They spotted *Ardent* but not the rest of the landing force. Though only a single ship was known to the Argentines, four flights of Daggers were sent against her. Meanwhile a reconnaissance pilot from Stanley found the rest of the British force in San Carlos water and five more groups of strike aircraft were quickly dispatched.

The first waves arrived over the course of 20 minutes. Of 11 Daggers, one was shot down by a Sea Slug missile while HMS *Antrim* took a bomb hit which struck the missile magazine but failed to explode. *Broadsword* and *Antrim* were also strafed with cannon fire. Two hours went by before the next attack, allowing the British to get more supplies landed.

The next attack consisted of a single Skyhawk, as two of its flight returned to base with mechanical problems and the third mistakenly attacked an abandoned Argentine freighter beached nearby. That Skyhawk attacked *Ardent* but missed; the only damage came from the Skyhawk

RIGHT: This famous image shows HMS *Invincible* returning to the UK to a joyous welcome after the crisis. British citizens were generally supportive of the hard-won conflict, which restored pride during the post-colonial era. UK MoD Crown Copyright

RIGHT: HMS *Invincible* steams in the Exclusion Zone, with two Sea Harriers spotted on her flight deck. Ken Griffiths

pilot clipping the ship's radar mast as he flew over. The Harrier CAP arrived too late to catch the pilot, who made his escape, but were on time to intercept the next wave of four Skyhawks. The Argentines jettisoned their bombs upon spotting the Harriers, but two planes were lost to Sidewinders.

After another lull which enabled even more supplies to reach the beach, a mixed force of Daggers and Skyhawks, including Argentine Navy A-4Qs, appeared in the afternoon of May 21. The first attack of four Daggers lost one plane to a Sidewinder from the CAP but continued toward their targets. Five Skyhawks came next, hitting *Argonaut* with two bombs which failed to explode but still did heavy »

BELOW: Helicopters pass by the destroyer HMS *Exeter* shortly after hostilities ended. Tim Jones

ABOVE: A GR3 Harrier at Stanley Airport. Inoperable Argentine aircraft are in the background. UK MoD Crown Copyright

BELOW: A Sea Dart missile launched from HMS *Invincible*. Though not perfect, the system downed seven Argentine aircraft during the Falklands Crisis. Ken Griffiths

damage, including the detonation of missiles in the frigate's magazine. Despite the damage, *Argonaut* stayed in the San Carlos Water for nine days, lending her firepower to the battle.

The three surviving Daggers arrived simultaneously with another flight of three Daggers and two flights of Skyhawks. None of their bombs hit but *Broadsword* and *Brilliant* were strafed. The CAP intercepted a third flight of Daggers, downing all of them. HMS *Ardent*, however bore the brunt of six A-4Q Skyhawks. Flying low between hills to mask their approach, the Argentine pilots scored six or seven bomb hits on *Ardent*, most on the stern. The vessel sank in shallow water after the surviving crew abandoned ship. At the end of May 21, the Royal Navy had lost a frigate while the Argentines lost 10 aircraft.

Weather conditions over Argentina prevented attacks on May 22, but they resumed 24 hours later. More British support ships arrived to offload cargo, escorted by HMS *Antelope*. Skyhawk attacks hit *Antelope*, but the bombs failed to explode. The next few sorties scored no hits but lost one plane to the CAP. Bomb disposal specialists tried to defuse the bombs imbedded in *Antelope*, but one exploded, starting fires and forcing the crew to abandon. The ship sank the next morning after a large explosion.

The Argentines changed their direction of approach on May 24, giving the British force less time to engage. They also switched their focus to the landing ships and transports, although this was too late as most of the stores were already ashore. The logistics landing ships *Sir Galahad* and *Sir Lancelot* both suffered bomb hits for the loss of four Argentine planes.

Heavy Argentine attacks came in on May 25, their National Day. The initial attacks achieved little other than the loss of three aircraft. One damaged Skyhawk leaked fuel so badly it returned home only by staying connected to a refuelling plane which kept pumping fuel into its rapidly draining fuel tanks. In the afternoon, the Argentines attacked HMS *Coventry* and *Broadsword*, steaming near Pebble Island. These ships had been using their radars to guide the CAP and their Sea Dart missiles to down attacking aircraft. Once the Argentine command realised this, they sent four Skyhawks to attack the ships. The first two Skyhawks again came in low, which prevented Sea Dart from locking on to them. Their bombs missed, though one bounced off the water onto *Broadsword's* helicopter deck, taking the nose off a Lynx before punching through the deck and into the sea. The ship's missile systems again failed to acquire the second pair of Skyhawks, which landed three bombs on *Coventry*, two of which caused rapid flooding. Within 15 minutes the ship lay on her side in the water, sinking soon after.

The next attack proved one of the most serious of the war. Two Exocet-equipped Super Êtendards attempted to attack the carrier group, which had moved west to cover the landings and HMS *Coventry*. The pilots again flew low but had to ascend briefly to gain a missile lock. They saw three targets on their radar, one larger than the others, so they fired on it. Rather than a carrier, it was *Atlantic Conveyor*, a large STUFT transport carrying most of the landing force's helicopters and other vital supplies. One missile seemed distracted by a chaff cloud fired by *Ambuscade* but appeared to acquire the STUFT vessel afterward. One or both missiles hit the ship, starting fires which quickly grew unmanageable. Within a half hour it became obvious the *Atlantic Conveyor* would be lost. Twelve sailors died, with the rest lifted off by helicopters or in life rafts. The ship burned out but stayed afloat for a few days before sinking on May 28.

Much of the Argentine air effort switched to targets on land as it was now clear the British ground force was the major threat to Argentina's hold on the islands. The CAP continued against these attacks, now bolstered by a small airfield ashore that allowed refuelling. The second wave of ground forces arrived during the last few days of May, bringing

LEFT: Two Sea Harriers from 800 Naval Air Squadron, which flew from HMS *Hermes* during the crisis. US Navy

LEFT: The amphibious logistics ship RFA *Sir Lancelot*. Such ships were vital to getting the ground forces ashore and keeping them supplied. IWM MH27593

an infantry brigade and supporting units. *Hermes* used its GR3 Harriers to attack Argentine ground defences, significantly reducing Argentine capabilities and affecting morale.

The frigates and destroyers took part in shore bombardment missions in addition to task force defence. A land-based Exocet just missed *Avenger*, and Argentine artillery gradually got better at firing on moving ships offshore, prompting the bombardment vessels to stay farther out to sea. The nuclear submarines, instrumental in keeping the Argentine surface fleet in port, also acted as pickets along the Argentine coast, reporting outgoing aircraft.

On May 28, the Argentines used their last air-launched Exocet in an attempt to strike a British carrier, but in fact engaged the frigate HMS *Avenger*. The missile was supposed to strike the carrier and four Skyhawks would follow the missile in and attack with bombs. The Exocet missed altogether, and *Avenger* brought down two Skyhawks with missiles and gunfire. The second two Skyhawks dropped their bombs and retired, claiming they had struck a carrier, but *Invincible* was miles away. Nevertheless, it was a well-planned and daring attack.

The last major Argentine success of the war came on June 8, when five Daggers found HMS *Plymouth* on a bombardment mission outside the British air defence envelope. Four bombs struck the ship; though none exploded, one set off one of the ship's depth charges, starting a fire. The crew extinguished the flames within 90 minutes, and the ship returned to San Carlos. A flight of Skyhawks managed to penetrate British defences and reach Bluff Cove, an inlet south of Stanley, where troops were landing for the final ground operations. Their bombs struck two landing support ships, *Sir Galahad* and *Sir Tristram*, causing fires on *Sir Galahad* which burned the ship out. A follow up attack sank one landing craft but three Skyhawks fell to the CAP. On June 11, *Glamorgan* took damage from a shore-fired Exocet during a bombardment mission. Aside from a few more air attacks, the naval portion of the war wound to a close and Argentine ground forces surrendered at Stanley on June 14.

Both sides fought with determination and courage, though Argentina was handicapped by a lack of aerial refuelling capacity which limited the size of air attacks. Flying low reduced their aircraft losses but failed to allow their bombs time to arm, causing many duds. The Sea Harriers and their advanced Sidewinder missiles were a marked success, and while the British air defence scheme didn't function perfectly, it was good enough to protect the carriers and landing force from grievous harm, allowing them to accomplish their mission. The Argentine surface fleet stayed in port, reasonably concerned about British nuclear submarines. The Royal Navy lost 86 sailors during the conflict along with another 18 civilian sailors. Argentina lost 341 sailors, most on the *Belgrano*, while their air force lost 31 pilots. The lessons learned during the war still influence naval, carrier and air defence operations to this day.

BELOW: HMS *Yarmouth* and HMS *Andromeda* steam behind HMS *Cardiff* in the South Atlantic. The cold, rough seas and harsh weather took their toll on ships and crew. Ken Griffiths

OPERATION PRAYING MANTIS 1988

The US Navy's one day war against Iran

On April 14, 1988, the frigate USS *Samuel B. Roberts* struck an Iranian sea mine in the Persian Gulf while en route to refuel with the USS *San Jose*. The frigate had transited the area a few days earlier without encountering any mines. The mine blasted a 15ft hole in the ship's hull and broke her keel. Usually, such damage guarantees the loss of the ship, but crew managed to control the fires and flooding, keeping the ship afloat. US Navy (USN) divers found several more mines in the area and recovered them for investigation. The mine's serial numbers were in sequence with other mines found aboard an Iranian minelayer which the USN had boarded seven months earlier.

At the time, the USN maintained extensive forces in the Persian Gulf region due to the various ongoing crises. These included US tensions with Iran and the war between Iran and Iraq, which was interfering with oil shipments. Operation Earnest Will, a mission to escort reflagged oil tankers, had been underway since July 1987. USN forces in the area included the aircraft carrier USS *Enterprise* and a large number of cruisers, destroyers and frigates.

This gave the USN extensive assets for use in Operation Praying Mantis, designed to discourage Iran from continuing its minelaying activities and attacks on ships in the Gulf. Three Surface Action Groups (SAGs) received assignments to attack different Iranian targets. Carrier aircraft from *Enterprise* would support each group as needed.

The operation began at 8:04 on April 18, 1988 with an attack on the Sassan oil platform, which the Iranians used as a base of operations. SAG Bravo consisted of the destroyers USS *Merrill* and USS *Lynde McCormick*, along with the amphibious transport USS *Trenton* carrying a Marine task force with helicopters, commanded by Captain James Perkins. As the group approached the platform, Perkins signalled: "You have five minutes to abandon the platform, I intend to destroy it at 0800 hours." Two tugs that were docked at the platform soon left, but some Iranians stayed behind, manning a 23mm cannon. In the event, Capt Perkins waited nine

BELOW: The USS *Samuel B. Roberts* is carried out of the Gulf for repairs by the Dutch recovery ship *Mighty Servant 2*. An Omani fast attack craft escorts them. US Navy

minutes, announced their time was up and the SAG opened fire.

The first salvo used airbursts to destroy antennae and pin down the defenders. The 23mm gun started firing but was quickly silenced by a direct hit from *Merrill*'s 5in guns. After gunfire covered the southern half of the platform, the remaining Iranians gathered at the northern side and the SAG ceased fire while a tug returned to pick them up, after which the shelling resumed. At 09:25 a Marine boarding force landed on the platform under covering fire from Cobra attack helicopters. After searching the platform for useful intelligence, the Marines planted explosives and withdrew. The demolition charges reduced the platform to a burning wreck.

SAG Bravo set course north for its next target, the Rakhish platform. One of the Cobras spotted a warship, tentatively identified as an Iranian frigate approaching at 25kts. Merrill made ready to fire Harpoon missiles, but Perkins asked for more information to confirm the ship's identity. It turned out to be a Soviet destroyer; when the Americans asked what the Soviets intended, their captain replied: "I want to take pictures for history." SAG Bravo was soon diverted to investigate reports of

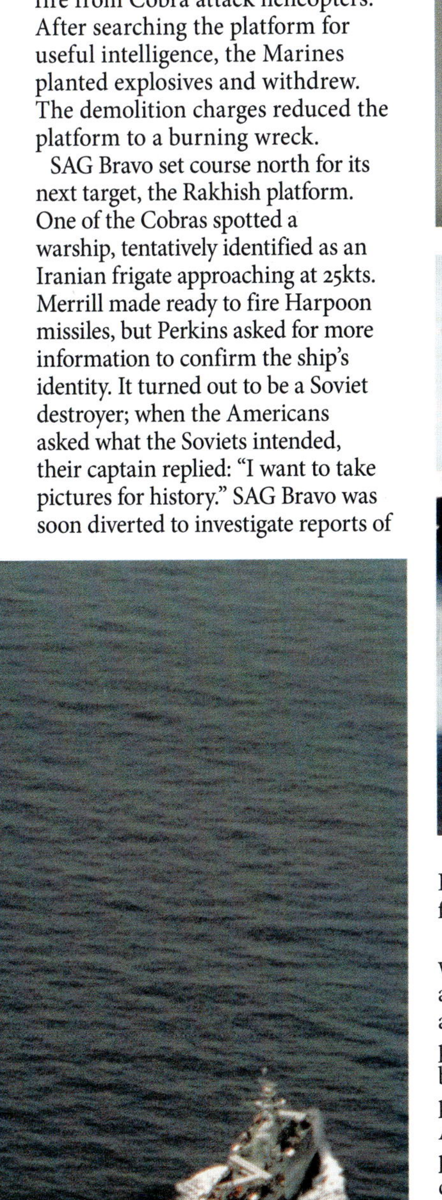

Iranian small boats nearby and took no further part in the overall operation.

A pair of A-6E Intruders dealt with the small boats first. Known almost generically as 'Boghammers' after a Swedish speedboat design purchased by the Iranians, these boats were reportedly firing on oil platforms crewed by Americans. Arriving overhead, the pilots received permission to engage; each plane carried a Harpoon missile, a cluster bomb and a Laser Guided Bomb (LGB). Each plane dropped their Rockeye cluster bombs, which spread bomblets across an area the size of a football pitch.

At least two Boghammers suffered damage and the boats withdrew, observed by the Intruder crews. Flight leader Lieutenant Jim Engler recalled the Iranians had: "headed back to their base at Abu Musa Island – they drove their Boghammers right up onto the beach. The crews literally ran out the front of them and hid in the sand on the shore, while we flew above them watching it happen. We had done what we needed to do."

Just a few minutes after SAG Bravo began its mission, SAG Charlie under Captain James Chandler attacked the Sirri-D oil platforms. Composed of the cruiser USS *Wainwright* and frigates USS *Simpson* and USS *Bagley*, the SAG began shelling the platform and soon detected an approaching Iranian warship, the *Joshan*, a French-built fast attack craft equipped with Harpoon missiles, a few of which had been delivered to Iran before the revolution stopped arms transfers. The SAG also detected a pair of Iranian F-4 Phantom fighters circling about 35 miles away.

A helicopter sent to confirm *Joshan's* identity soon received challenges to withdraw accompanied by »

ABOVE: An A-7E Corsair II prepares to launch from USS *Enterprise* during the operation. Six Corsairs took part in the destruction of the Iranian frigate IS *Sahand.* US Navy

TOP: An A-6E Intruder from USS *Enterprise* drops a CBU-59 Rockeye cluster bomb on an Iranian target during the operation. Note the bomb casing has opened to dispense its submunitions. US Navy

RIGHT: The Iranian frigate IS *Sabalan* underway in the Gulf, 1977. Built by Vosper, they were equipped for surface, anti-air and anti-submarine warfare. US Navy

RIGHT: IS *Sahand*, sister ship to *Sabalan*, underway in the Gulf. The ship took multiple hits from missiles and bombs, sinking with a few hours. US Navy

threats it would be shot down. *Bagley's* captain radioed: "We are a US Navy warship, and if you fire on our helicopter, we will sink you." The helicopter crew confirmed *Joshan's* identity and that it was carrying a Harpoon launcher.

Soon after, *Joshan* fired a missile and SAG Charlie deployed chaff and other countermeasures. SAG Charlie broadcast: "Abandon ship, we intend to sink you." The US ships launched five Standard SM-1 missiles, loaded for their dual anti-aircraft/anti-ship capabilities due to the nearby F-4s. The first supersonic SM-1 hit *Joshan* before the subsonic Harpoon flew past *Wainwright*, only 100ft away. Two more SM-1s hit, wrecking *Joshan's* superstructure and starting fires, but it remained afloat.

The F-4s were engaged with SM-2 missiles, damaging one aircraft, and both withdrew. The American ships were now in visual range and detected an electronic emission from *Joshan*. USS *Simpson* fired another SM-1 which hit and the *Bagley* also fired a Harpoon. Incredibly, observers watched it pass through a hole torn in the *Joshan's* superstructure and continue on without exploding. The SAG finished off the stricken ship with gunfire.

Less than an hour later, the Iranian frigate *Sahand* departed the port at Bandar Abbas and was detected by a USN E-2C Hawkeye. SAG Delta, consisting of the destroyers USS *O'Brien* and *Joseph Strauss* and frigate USS *Jack Williams*, responded to search for the Iranian vessel. The SAG wanted the *Sahand* to get a little farther from shore to avoid confusing the tracking system of the Harpoon missile.

As they waited, an A-6E Intruder crew spotted *Sahand* as it moved to open sea. Due to the perpetual sandy haze which covers the Persian Gulf, they flew in for a visual identification. Passing the ship at 500kts, 50ft altitude and only 150ft away, Sahand's crew fired machine guns at the Intruder and launched several handheld SA-7 SAMs (Western embargoes had left Iran depleted of other missiles, so ship's crews used shoulder fired SAMs instead). The Americans launched chaff and manoeuvred, avoiding the missiles, then informed their air controller they had been fired upon and were attacking. The US pilot switched his radio to the Iranian

BELOW: The IS *Sahand* being struck by US Navy bombs. The image appears to be from an infrared or thermal imaging camera. US Navy

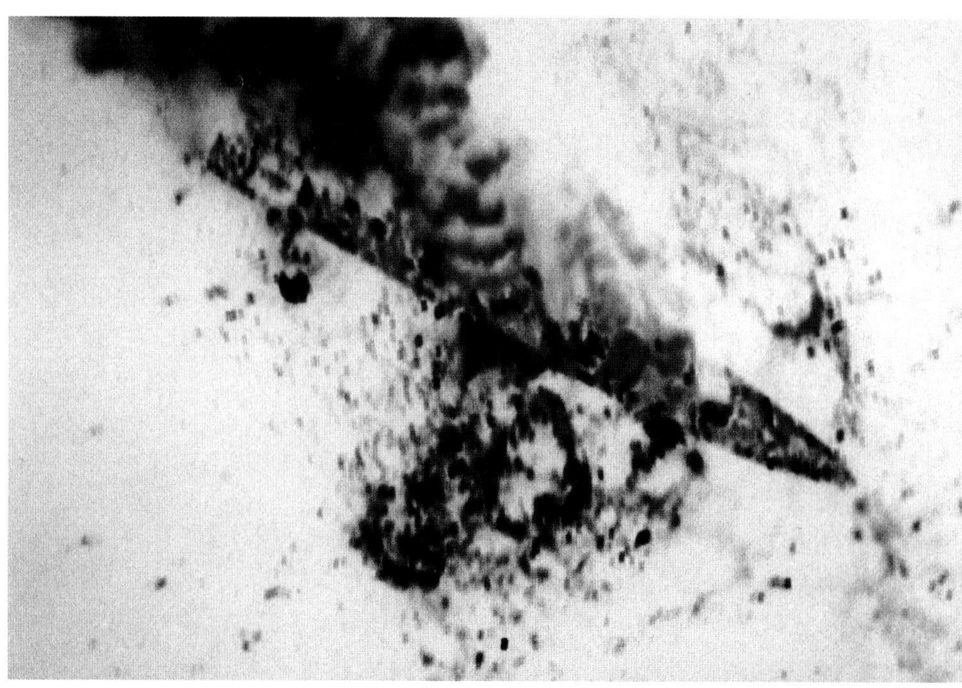

ABOVE: IS *Sahand* reduced to a burning wreck by a combination of Harpoon missiles and cluster bombs. US Navy

frequency and warned: "I am going to sink you in five minutes."

The A-6E fired a Harpoon from eight miles out and the missile hit just aft of the bridge, starting a large fire. *Sahand* soon went dead in the water. They next fired two Skipper missiles, basically a 1,000lb bomb with a rocket motor, and one hit the frigate. Out of ordnance, the A-6E stayed overhead to direct in the next wave of aircraft comprising another A-6E and six A-7E Corsairs. The Intruder fired a Harpoon along with another launched by the *Joseph Strauss*. Both missiles appeared to hit, and the A-6 lined up for a shot with a Skipper. The bombardier put his laser on the ship's stern, which had not been hit yet. The Skipper struck its aimpoint, causing a large explosion.

The A-6 lined up to drop a laser-guided bomb (LGB), but the bombardier chose to call off the attack. *Sahand* was aflame from stem to stern and the crew was abandoning ship. He later said: "Our job was not to kill the sailors who were clearly just abandoning ship. That's not the way we do business, so I made the decision not to release those final weapons." *Sahand* sank a few hours later.

The frigate *Sabalan*, sister ship to *Sahand*, had also departed Bandar Abbas and hid among the heavy Gulf shipping traffic. Some US sailors had hoped to engage *Sabalan*, due to the prior actions of its commander, Abdollah Manavi, who had a reputation for firing on civilian ships and broadcasting "have a nice day" via radio afterwards. Now he played a game of cat and mouse with the US Navy.

A prowling A-6E found *Sabalan* and the frigate opened fire with guns and missiles. The Intruder dove on the ship, launching one LGB which flew straight down the ship's stack and exploded in the engine room. *Sabalan* stopped, then slowly turned toward Bandar Abbas, leaving a huge oil slick behind it. As the USS *Jack Williams* approached to launch a Harpoon, the Iranians fired several Silkworm missiles from coastal defences, so the frigate turned away, using chaff and electronic systems to avoid being hit.

An A-6 lined up to fire a Harpoon at *Sabalan* when Captain Manavi got a reprieve straight from Washington DC. The US Administration felt their point had been made and ordered Operation Praying Mantis to an end. Several tugs towed *Sabalan* back to port, where she was repaired and still serves in the Iranian Navy today. Manavi eventually rose to the rank of vice admiral in the Iranian Navy. After temporary repairs in Dubai, the USS *Samuel B. Roberts* returned to the United States for full repairs and served until 2015.

RIGHT: Part of the Sassan oil platform burns after being struck by a TOW missile from a US Marine Corps Cobra attack helicopter. US Navy

NAVAL POWER IN THE GLOBAL WAR ON TERRORISM

Airpower, cruise missiles and logistics

RIGHT: A Royal Navy boat crew escorts an Iraqi small boat at the port of Um Qasr in 2008. Securing Iraq's exclusive economic zone was a major goal toward rebuilding the nation's economy. US Navy

The war against international terrorism entered a dramatic new phase after the 9/11 attacks on the United States in 2001. The previous year the destroyer USS *Cole* was the target of a suicide attack while the ship was in Aden to refuel. The attack, carried out using a small boat packed with explosives, resulted in the deaths of 17 US Navy sailors and injury to a further 39 personnel. Attributed to al-Qaeda, the attack was seen as the precursor to 9/11 and as well as the human toll, caused extensive damage to the warship.

Military operations in Afghanistan began soon after the 9/11 attacks with naval forces providing air power, transport and logistics support. The navies of the United States, Great Britain and France provided the majority of combat vessels and they were soon joined by other NATO members including Italy and Holland. In particular, the French nuclear-powered carrier *Charles De Gaulle*, commissioned only five months before the September 11 attacks, quickly deployed to Afghanistan to conduct air operations.

When military operations expanded to Iraq, aircraft carriers provided a large share of the strike aircraft used in both the initial invasion and subsequent counterinsurgency effort. US carriers would spend the next two decades rotating through combat deployments supporting operations in Iraq and Afghanistan. These operations continued against the so-called Islamic State (IS) until its defeat in 2019. Carrier aircraft continue to fly missions against IS remnants and other terrorist and proxy groups in the region.

Aircraft carriers acted as the primary method of projecting naval power ashore. Carriers possess endurance, as they carry large supplies of fuel and ordnance, as well as the maintenance facilities to keep their air wings operational for months at a time. Modern naval strike aircraft are also well-equipped with precision air to ground munitions and can loiter overhead for extended periods using air-to-air refuelling tankers. The aircraft carrier is also a mobile and relatively safe operating base. Operating from

BELOW: The destroyer USS *Cole* arrives at the Ingalls shipyard in Pascagoula, Mississippi for repairs after being damaged in a terrorist attack in Aden, Yemen in 2000. It is being carried by the Norwegian heavy lift ship *Blue Marlin*. US Navy

international waters, they don't require permission to operate within national territory as would land-based air forces. Terror groups generally lack the capabilities to attack a carrier at sea, with the exception of the Houthis and their ongoing missile and UAS campaign in the Red Sea (see page 82).

Counter-terror operations took place in other areas, such as Africa and other parts of the Middle East beyond Iraq and Afghanistan. For example, the US missile strike on Syria in 2017 used 59 Tomahawk cruise missiles launched from two destroyers striking an air base and its defences. A previous cruise missile attack, Operation Infinite Reach in 1998, sought to retaliate against al-Qaeda for its attacks on the US embassies in Kenya and Tanzania. Between 70 and 90 cruise missiles were fired from seven USN warships, including a submarine, but the mission achieved little and even emboldened al-Qaeda due to its relative ineffectiveness.

Naval power also proved effective in the amount of logistical support it provided. This included fuel, ordnance and military supplies, but also humanitarian aid. Such support gave naval forces staying power and supplied ground forces. Naval personnel, including intelligence specialists and electronic warfare technicians also deployed ashore. US Army and Marine troops, for example, lacked the skills and equipment to defeat some terrorist methods involving radio-detonated bombs and suicide vehicles. USN equipment provided essential jamming capabilities. Special forces units including Britain's Special Boat Squadron and US Navy SEAL teams also saw wide service in counterterror operations in a variety of locations.

The waters of the Middle East saw widespread naval activity designed to intercept and capture cargoes intended for terror groups use or support. This included arms shipments, narcotics, and other things which can be used to raise funding. The Combined Maritime Forces were established in 2002 to combat terrorism and piracy in the region. These forces are divided into four Combined Task Forces, numbered 150 through 153, each with its own mission or region of operation. These are multinational forces with command rotating through the participating countries and will likely continue to operate in the region for years or decades to come.

ABOVE: The logistics landing ship RFA *Sir Galahad* arrives in Um Qasr in 2003, carrying the first shipment of humanitarian aid to Iraq. *Sir Galahad* later served with the Brazilian Navy and was sunk as a target ship in 2019. US Navy

LEFT: USS *Enterprise* in the North Arabian Sea supporting Operation Enduring Freedom in Afghanistan, 2007. Naval air power was the US Navy's primary contribution to the operations in Iraq and Afghanistan. US Navy

BELOW: The frigate HMS *Richmond* patrols the waters near the Al Basra oil terminal in 2009. Note the haze which frequently covers the Persian Gulf. US Navy

WAR IN THE BLACK SEA

Russian naval power versus Ukrainian innovation

BELOW: A Russian ship of the Black Sea Fleet fires chaff and smoke during an exercise. Such countermeasures can distract an anti-ship missile as it nears its target. Russian MoD

When Russia invaded Ukraine on February 24, 2022, no informed observer would have predicted anything but complete Russian success and freedom of action against the tiny Ukrainian Navy. However, against the odds, the Ukrainian military, despite possessing little more than a handful of patrol boats and coastal forces has managed to take the fight to the Russian invaders. Both combatants have delivered effective attacks against the other and while neither side has been decisively defeated, the Ukrainians have managed to keep the Russian Navy at bay, reducing its effectiveness and its ability to support Russian troops ashore.

Ukraine's success in the Black Sea is primarily due to the innovative use of existing and new technologies. This includes sea drones, use of UAS and cruise missiles, a willingness to experiment with novel methods of employment as well as combining different systems to work in concert. As in the land campaign, initial Russian plans for their operation proved optimistic or inaccurate.

Stiff fighting along the Ukrainian coast began on the first day of the invasion. The Russian Navy planned to land two amphibious task forces of naval infantry along the coast between Kherson and Odessa to capture key points. This would enable advancing Russian ground forces to quickly advance toward Odessa, securing the entire Ukrainian coastline. However, when Russian special forces in small boats attempted to land and carry out reconnaissance, they were engaged and defeated by Ukrainian coastal defences which forced a cancellation of the landings.

One Russian success on the first day was the capture of the Ukrainian-held Snake Island, although the Ukrainians gained a propaganda victory when their small garrison showed defiance. When the Russian cruiser *Moskva* called on them via radio to surrender, the Ukrainian border guards on the island replied: "Russian warship, go f**k yourself." This quickly became a rallying cry and although Ukraine believed the borders guards had been killed in the subsequent attack, they were actually taken prisoner and later exchanged.

A few days later a squadron of small boats of the Ukrainian Navy attacked Russian naval forces around the island. In March, the Ukrainians damaged a Russian patrol boat using an anti-tank missile. They also managed to sink a Russian landing ship in Berdiansk harbour, captured by the Russians a month earlier.

As the Russians began to establish defences on Snake Island, Ukraine responded. On April 14, the Russian Black Sea Fleet flagship *Moskva* sank after being struck by two R-360 Neptune anti-ship cruise missiles, a Ukrainian design which had just entered service. Some reports indicate that one or more Bayraktar TB2 drones were used to distract the ship's crew from the impending missile strike or provided targeting information. This major loss caused the Russians to pull their ships farther from the coast.

Over the following month TB2s attacked several Russian ships and the defences being set up on the island. Several patrol boats and landing craft were damaged, though claims of losses on each side differ. On June 17, the Ukrainians used Harpoon missiles to sink a Russian tug bringing supplies to the island, but Russian air defence systems shot down two Ukrainian Su-24s a week later. However, the Russian occupation of the island became untenable, and they withdrew their forces on June 30.

Despite these setbacks, the Russian Navy remained a threat to Ukraine, as its frigates and corvettes carried the Kalibr cruise missile, with a range of 1,500km, which meant they could be launched beyond the range of Ukrainian shore-based anti-ship missiles. These ships carried out regular attacks as part of Russia's overall aerial bombardment campaign against Ukrainian infrastructure, industry and military targets. While the Ukrainian air defence network has proven able to intercept many of the incoming missiles, enough got through to cause considerable damage to the country's electrical grid and other vital resources.

In response, as the war continued with no sign of a ceasefire, Ukraine carefully employed its small number of long-range munitions, most supplied by the West, against Russian ships and port facilities on the Crimean Peninsula at Sevastopol. On September 23, 2023, an attack »

ABOVE: A Magura unmanned surface vehicle approaching the Russian ship *Ivan Khurs* during an attack. This is a still from video recorded by the Magura's onboard camera; in the video it appears to strike the Russian ship. Ukrainian MoD

LEFT: The Russian frigate *Admiral Essen* launches a surface to air missile at a Ukrainian Bayraktar UAS in April 2022. The ship also carries launch tubes for the *Kalibr* cruise missile. Russian MoD

ABOVE: The Russian cruiser *Moskva* served as flagship of the Black Sea Fleet and took part in the attack on Snake Island at the beginning of the war. Russian MoD

using Storm Shadow missiles hit the Black Sea Fleet headquarters in that city, also damaging a submarine and landing ship. Though often not thought of as important targets compared to combatant warships, amphibious landing ships have been a major concern for Ukraine. Their destruction reduces the chance of a Russian landing along their coastline and hampers Russian efforts to keep ground forces supplied in the occupied portions of Southern Ukraine.

As Ukraine lacks the ability to project sea power away from its coastline, they made use of a new innovation, the sea drone or Unmanned Surface Vehicle (USV).

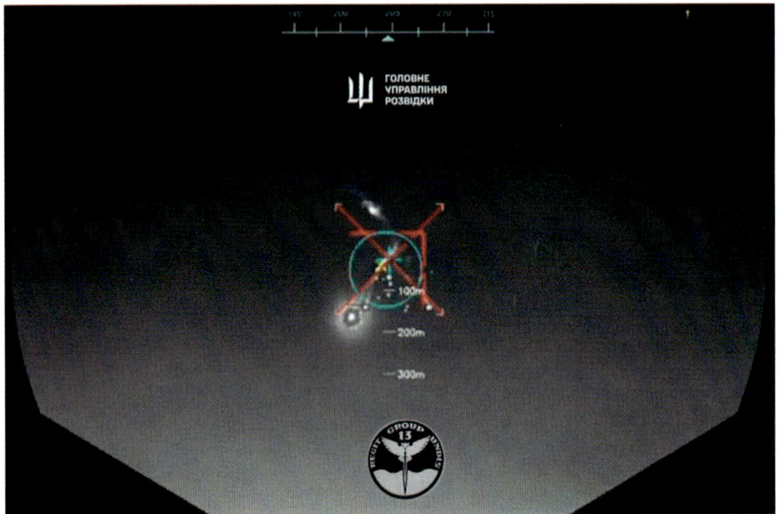

RIGHT: A still shot from video of a Ukrainian Magura sea drone shooting down a Russian SU-30 strike aircraft with a Sidewinder missile. Ukrainian MoD – Intelligence Directorate

RIGHT: *Moskva* burning after a Ukrainian strike using two R-360 Neptune land-based anti-ship missiles. The ship later sank while under tow. Russian MoD

While USVs were already seeing wider use globally, the Ukrainians made them into armed offensive weapons. The initial versions functioned as 'kamikaze' weapons, ramming Russian ships to detonate an explosive payload.

One version nicknamed the 'Sea Baby,' carried a warhead of up to 850kg and saw one of its first combat uses against the bridge over the Kerch Strait, connecting Crimea to the Russian mainland. This was part of a dedicated Ukrainian campaign against the bridge, which is used to transport supplies to the Russian military in Crimea. Another type, the Maritime Autonomous Guard Unmanned Robotic Apparatus (MAGURA), carries a smaller warhead and is more manoeuvrable, making it more effective against moving ships.

These USVs are relatively inexpensive (a Sea Baby costs in the region of $200-250,000) and can be mass-produced. Many are purchased using crowd-funding efforts. Attacks against Russian warships both in port and at sea became frequent occurrences, with footage from the USV's onboard camera often posted online, particularly when they obtained a hit. Attacking USVs can be engaged with shipboard weapons or strafed by aircraft and helicopters. Even a 7.62mm machine gun can knock a USV out of action or destroy it, but attacks by large numbers of USVs can overwhelm a ship's defences.

The effectiveness of these Ukrainian efforts forced the Russian Navy to pull its ships back from Sevastopol to the Russian mainland port of Novorossiysk. There, they can be more easily defended and are out of range of most of Ukraine's limited number of long-range munitions. This has not stopped the Russian Navy from operating in the Black Sea but it has forced them to be more careful and deliberate in their operations.

By mid-2024, Ukraine made the further innovation of mounting weapons on their USVs, including .50 calibre machine guns and infrared seeking anti-aircraft missiles. These weapons have been used to engage aircraft as they attack USV groups. In late December 2024, a MAGURA shot down a Russian Mi-8 helicopter and damaged another, using modified R-73 missiles. In May 2025, Ukraine reported downing a pair of Russian Su-30s using Sidewinder missiles from a MAGURA. It was the first time a USV had shot down a jet aircraft in combat.

While the Russian Black Sea Fleet maintains some combat power, its effectiveness has been greatly decreased by Ukrainian use of USVs and missiles. As of writing, the independent website Oryx lists 21 Russian ships destroyed and seven damaged, including one cruiser, three corvettes, one submarine, and seven landing ships and craft. Ukrainian ship losses include 14 vessels destroyed and 19 captured, most of those in the first days of the war. The majority of Ukrainian losses are patrol boats and other small craft. Its largest ship, an ageing frigate, was scuttled to prevent capture at the beginning of the war.

With war still ongoing, accurate counts of ship losses cannot be entirely relied on, as both sides make claims about their successes and enemy failures. This is a normal part of the chaos and propaganda of war. It will be years before the true losses are known. Whatever the effects, they are nevertheless considerable and point toward the future of naval warfare in the use of long-range weapons, USVs, UAS and armed robotic weapons.

ABOVE: Ukraine has also made extensive efforts to strike Russian amphibious warfare ships to prevent a landing on their coast and hinder Russian resupply efforts for their ground forces. Russian MoD

BELOW: The Ukrainian R-360 Neptune anti-ship missile has had some success against Russian warships. It has a range of 300km, enough to keep Russian ships well away from the coast. Ukrainian MoD

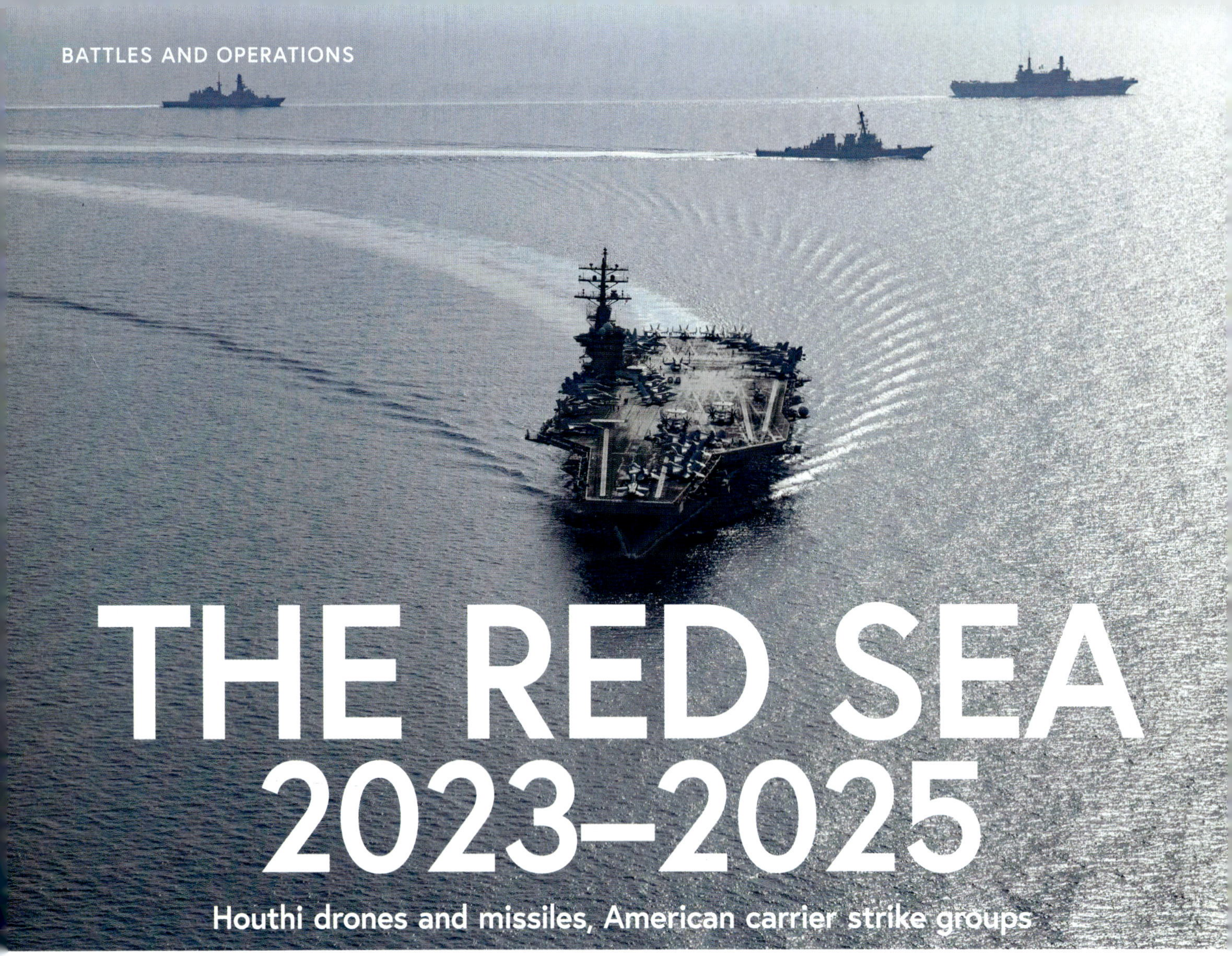

THE RED SEA 2023–2025

Houthi drones and missiles, American carrier strike groups

The attack by Hamas on Israel which began on October 7, 2023, quickly escalated into a wider conflict. In response to the Gaza war, the United States dispatched the carrier strike groups (CSGs) centred on the aircraft carriers USS *Gerald R. Ford* and USS *Dwight D. Eisenhower* to the eastern Mediterranean. The Houthis, an Iranian-backed militant movement, declared support for Hamas and soon began firing missiles and drones at Israel and attacking merchant ships in the Red Sea. Houthi control of western Yemen put them in position to fire on ships in the Red Sea and the Gulf of Aden, using ballistic and cruise missiles along with drones and loitering munitions.

The first Houthi attacks began on October 19, 2023, with missiles and drones aimed at Israel. That same day the destroyer USS *Carney* shot down four Houthi cruise missiles and 15 drones during a nine-hour period. Houthi attacks intensified over the following weeks and in mid-November, Houthi fighters used helicopters to board and hijack the merchant ship *Galaxy Leader*. The crew of 25 were held hostage until January 2025.

In mid-October the *Bataan* amphibious ready group ships USS *Bataan*, an amphibious assault ship and USS *Carter Hall*, a dock landing ship, were diverted from the Persian Gulf to the Red Sea. *Bataan's* air group included USMC Harrier fighters and AH-1Y Cobra attack helicopters. Once on station these aircraft began patrols and as other warships arrived, including the USS *Arleigh Burke*, they established engagement zones to facilitate the interception of Houthi missiles and drones.

The Marines aboard *Bataan* modified one of the Harriers for air defence, enabling it to carry more missiles than normal. *Arleigh Burke* used its advanced radar to detect Houthi launches, directing the Harriers and ships for interception. Marine pilot Captain Earl Ehrhart received credit for intercepting seven Houthi drones in a Harrier.

Houthi attacks continued, prompting the United States to launch Operation Prosperity Guardian in December, designed to protect ships in the region from Houthi attacks. Most of the ships

ABOVE: USS *Eisenhower* steams with USS *Laboon* in the Red Sea, June 2024, accompanied by the Italian carrier *Cavour* and frigate *Alpino*. Protecting shipping in the region quickly became a multinational effort. US Navy

LEFT: A USMC Harrier aboard USS *Bataan* in the Red Sea, August 2023. Harriers optimised for air defence had success against Houthi drones. USMC

Another major attack occurred on January 9, 2024 with US and British forces downing a reported 21 Houthi drones and missiles. This marked the beginning of what became known as the 'Battle of the BAM,' an acronym for the Bab-el-Mandeb Strait. HMS *Diamond* of the Royal Navy took part in the action, firing Aster missiles at the incoming missiles and drones. The American destroyers fired Standard missiles while Eisenhower's Super Hornets use the new AIM9X Block II Sidewinder missile.

Three days later those same Anglo-American forces commenced Operation Poseidon Archer, a combination of airstrikes and cruise missile attacks designed to degrade the Houthi's ability to continue its attacks. *Eisenhower's* Super Hornets and RAF »

ABOVE: On March 6, 2024, a Houthi anti-ship ballistic missile struck the merchant vessel *True Confidence*, killing three sailors. Another missile struck the merchant ship *MSC Sky II*, while a third was shot down by USS *Carney*. US Navy

LEFT: USS *Gravely* fires a Tomahawk Land Attack Missile (TLAM) at a Houthi target, January 11, 2024. US Navy

BELOW: An F/A-18F Super Hornet takes off from USS *Eisenhower* on April 4, 2024. US fighters served as defensive interceptors and flew strike missions against Houthi military installations. US Navy

and aircraft used in the operation were provided by the US and British navies along with a Sri Lankan patrol vessel and personnel support from several other nations. In late December *Bataan* and *Carter Hall* transited to the Mediterranean and CSG2 (USS *Eisenhower*) entered the Red Sea. Eisenhower escorts included the destroyers *Laboon*, *Gravely* and *Mason*.

The CSG went into action immediately; on December 26, Super Hornets from the carrier joined USS *Laboon* in destroying 12 drones and five missiles in a ten-hour engagement. Four days later, four Houthi boats attempted to put hijackers aboard the cargo ship *Maersk Hangzhou*, which had been struck by a Houthi missile. USN helicopters responded and were fired upon by the boats, so they returned fire, sinking three of them. As this was happening, the destroyer USS *Gravely* shot down two Houthi ballistic missiles.

ABOVE: A Super Hornet fires a chaff flare while manoeuvring over the Red Sea, January 2025. US Navy

RIGHT: USS Carney fires an interceptor missile at Houthi missiles and drones in October 2023. US Navy

Eurofighter Typhoons led the effort, dropping hundreds of air to surface weapons. Each phase of these operations received a nickname from US sailors, such as 'The Rumble in the Red Sea', or 'March Madness', which ended with over 36 drones shot down by Anglo-American forces. During some missions, *Eisenhower's* flight deck was completely empty, with only the Super Hornets in the hangar deck undergoing maintenance aboard ship.

The Houthis continued their campaign of shipping attacks while the US-UK-led coalition continued to strike Houthi launchers and air defences. USS *Eisenhower* used its E-2 Hawkeye early warning aircraft and E/A-18 Growler electronic warfare aircraft to detect Houthi attacks and coordinate interceptions as needed. The operation turned into a sustained battle, with *Eisenhower*'s air wing expending almost 500 munitions in interceptions and strikes before it left the area in June 2024.

After *Eisenhower's* departure, other USN forces also saw service during Operation Prosperity Guardian, including CSG 3 (USS *Abraham Lincoln*), CSG 8 (USS *Harry S. Truman*) and CSG 9 (USS *Theodore Roosevelt*). During the same period, the European Union enacted Operation Aspides, a purely defensive mission to protect shipping in the region. French, Italian, Greek, German, Dutch and Belgian ships have taken part, and have reportedly shot down at least 17 Houthi drones and missiles along with destroying two Houthi drone boats.

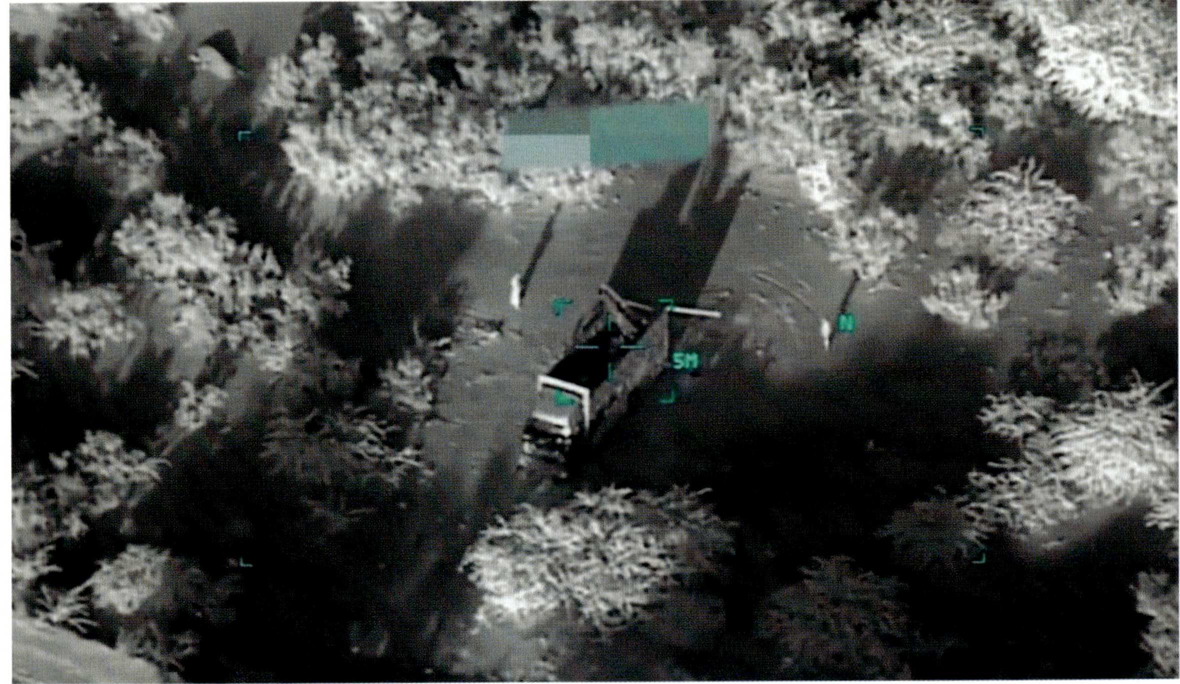

RIGHT: Drone footage of a Houthi missile launcher mounted on a truck, seconds before it was destroyed. US DoD

ABOVE: In this still from a video released by the Houthi movement, their commandos debark from a helicopter to seize the merchant ship Galaxy Leader in November 2023. Houthi news release

RIGHT: A Typhoon fighter of 903 Expeditionary Air Wing lands at RAF Akrotiri. Typhoon pilots flew missions against Houthi military targets using Storm Shadow missiles and Paveway IV bombs. UK MoD Crown Copyright

The US Navy reports the combat in the Red Sea to be the most sustained fighting it has seen since World War Two, in terms of ships at sea being targeted and engaged by air and missile attacks. By mid-March, 2025, US Central Command reported the Houthis had fired at US warships 170 times and civilian merchant vessels 145 times since the attacks began in 2023.

Alongside operations to defend shipping and degrade Houthi offensive capability, naval forces carried out an extensive campaign to curtail the flow of weapons to the Houthis from Iran and elsewhere. British Royal Marines, US Navy SEALs and others conducted boarding operations on vessels suspected of carrying weapons, munitions and equipment to the Houthis.

Beginning in March 2025, the US began Operation Rough Rider, a concerted campaign against Houthi military capability. The UK joined the effort the following month. The two nations flew hundreds of sorties, targeting communications nodes, drone and missile production facilities, fuel and ammunition depots and other military targets. As of writing, the US has announced a ceasefire with the Houthis though the situation is still chaotic and unpredictable.

RIGHT: The British and American aircraft which defended shipping in the Red Sea were kept operational through the efforts of hundreds of aircrew, who kept their strike fighters armed, fuelled and maintained. UK MoD Crown Copyright

PIRACY

The latest effort against an old problem

ABOVE: HMS *Cornwall's* Royal Marine boarding teams off the coast of Somalia in 2009. UK MoD Crown Copyright

Piracy remains a global problem in the 21st century. It dominates in economically strained regions where local nations lack the naval assets to effectively supress it. As the phenomenon has a strong economic basis, it cannot be eliminated, only managed. Piracy increases and recedes based on local conditions, opportunity and the amount of effort made to combat it.

In the last 20 years piracy around the Horn of Africa has drawn the most attention, but it flourishes in many other places, including the Gulf of Guinea (West Africa), Southeast Asia and South America. Most piracy occurs where shipping lanes and geography bring valuable cargo and even passenger vessels within reach of coastal areas that the pirates use as operating bases. A few also operate against oil pipelines and the companies which operate them.

Most pirate groups are small, independent organisations which are little more than criminal gangs. They generally seek to capture ships, crew and cargo which can be sold or ransomed. This involves extensive intelligence gathering in regional ports to select a suitable target, ideally a ship from a rich country but with with low sides and no defences to allow for easy boarding.

In Somalia, for example, tribal elders negotiate with a financial backer who puts up the money to purchase a support boat, two small fast boats for the attack and weapons for the pirates. Once a ship is seized the pirates turn off its communications, which essentially lets the ship's owners know it has been taken. Next, the ship is taken to a port and guarded. Communications are reestablished so negotiations can begin. Ransoms regularly exceed $5m per ship. The backer gets 60% of the money, with the rest going to the pirates and those they work with during the operation. Once released, the pirate's criminal network ensures the ship will not be retaken right away, as that would discourage future negotiation.

Most major naval powers contribute ships, usually destroyers, frigates and smaller ships, to antipiracy operations. Pirates are rarely willing to engage naval vessels and their boarding parties of trained and heavily armed marines and sailors. Naval task forces aim to capture pirates and turn them over to appropriate authorities for prosecution. Force is rarely needed. As political instability, climate change and economic hardships spread, piracy will continue to be problem for naval forces.

RIGHT: Sailors from the cruiser USS *Gettysburg* detain suspected pirates after responding to a distress call from a merchant ship in the Gulf of Aden, 2009. US Navy

THE FUTURE

Challenges old and new

The evolving global situation heralds changes to the existing order, increasing the likelihood of conflict. Control of the world's oceans is vital to commerce, resource extraction and food production, forcing competition. The years since 1945 have been generally peaceful at sea, allowing shipping to move about with little fear. During this period, the major guarantor of that freedom has been the United States Navy, ably supported by various allies. Together they enjoyed a naval supremacy that even the Soviet Union never seriously challenged.

That era of unchallenged supremacy is over. The rise of China as a global power with a rapidly expanding navy is the major factor in the changing environment. Russia, while no longer a strong naval power, is nonetheless a major player with extensive capabilities in certain areas. Iran and North Korea are really just regional spoilers, who could nonetheless cause major if temporary disruptions. It remains to be seen how other naval powers such as the United Kingdom, India and Japan will evolve in their interests and alliances in decades to come, particularly in regard to the changing political situation in the United States.

Technology also forces changes in future naval forces. Artificial intelligence, autonomous vessels, fifth and sixth generation aircraft and unmanned aerial systems are all in the early stages of development and use. How these technologies and others will change naval warfare can only be guessed at, with the pace of change quickening and new technologies growing obsolete before they are even fully employed.

What will not change is the need for alliances and military partnerships based on mutual interest and shared values. The US Navy remains the world's most powerful navy, but it cannot be strong everywhere. Its leaders recognise the need to work alongside allies; read almost any position paper or plan from the US Department of Defense and it will repeatedly state the need to plan and operate in cooperation with allies and partners. In a war against China, this is likely America's greatest advantage, as China has fewer potential allies, none of which can project naval power to any great degree.

It must be noted no such war is certain; the differences between China and its likely opponents could easily be solved peacefully. Perhaps the greatest threat is China's newfound power, for as nations grow rich and powerful they build a large military. The temptation to use it is hard to resist.

ABOVE: A grainy image of the Chinese carrier *Liaoning* conducting underway replenishment with a Type 901 fast combat support ship. The future for the Chinese Navy is one of growing global reach. Japan MoD

LEFT: The future for the Royal Navy and USN is in cooperation with allies. Here, Italian, German, American, French and British ships sail together as part of Task Force 150. US Navy

STRATEGIC WARFARE

Sea-launched nuclear weapons

Seaborne nuclear weapons will remain in widespread service for the foreseeable future. They are considered the most survivable of nuclear forces. Land-based weapons are either in hardened silos in fixed locations or on mobile launchers which can be found through reconnaissance, particularly before they are dispersed in response to a crisis. Even nuclear weapons carried by land-based aircraft must operate from fixed bases where the weapons can be properly stored and guarded. However, ships and submarines can move, making them much harder to find and target. This unpredictability adds to their deterrent effect. Nuclear weapons are deployable from numerous types of naval vessels.

LEFT: An artist's conception of the US Navy's Columbia-class ballistic missile submarine, expected to enter service in 2031. General Dynamics

Aircraft Carriers. Nuclear weapons have long been sufficiently miniaturised to enable their deployment by tactical strike aircraft like the F-35 Lightning, F/A-18 Super Hornet, and Rafale M. As aircraft can easily be modified with the specialised control and arming equipment for a nuclear weapon, it can be assumed Chinese, Indian and Russian carrier aircraft also are or can be quickly made nuclear capable as well. Russia's single carrier, *Kuznetsov*, is currently in poor repair and many experts doubt it will return to active duty. In October 2024, the Russian Navy transferred its crew to fight as ground troops in Ukraine, indicating it might never return to service.

BELOW: The Dreadnought-class will replace the Vanguard-class as the UK's nuclear deterrent in the early 2030s. UK MoD Crown Copyright

Cruise Missiles. A wide array of surface combatant ships and attack submarines carry cruise missiles, which have been used in numerous military operations in the last three decades. Many cruise missile designs are nuclear capable, such as the US Tomahawk and Russian Kalibr. When the Cold War ended, nuclear cruise missiles largely faded from use, along with a general reduction in tactical nuclear weapons. Now, with worldwide tensions increasing and the end of the Intermediate-Range Nuclear Forces (INF) Treaty, nuclear-tipped cruise missiles are once again proliferating.

The United States, for example, is funding development of the Sea-Launched Cruise Missile – Nuclear (SLCM-N). Few details of the weapon are available, but the effort signals a return to a more proliferated nuclear weapons policy. Supporters argue the weapons provide a lower-level response during a conflict than using larger, strategic weapons.

Submarines. The ballistic missile submarine, commonly identified by its US Navy acronym SSBN or the nickname 'Boomer,' is the major naval nuclear weapons delivery system for nuclear powers. The UK, France, China, India, Russia and the United States all operate ballistic missile submarines. For the UK and France, they are the primary nuclear deterrent force, although the French can operate nuclear cruise missile-equipped Rafale M fighters from their carrier. Submarines provide the best blend of survivability, stealth and speed to deliver their payloads of 12-20 Sea-Launched ballistic Missiles (SLBM) off an enemy's coast.

All these powers have a programme in place to replace their existing ballistic missile submarines with new designs as their current models reach the end of their service lives. Britain's Dreadnought, America's Columbia and China's Type 096 classes will all enter service in the 2030s. Each will carry missiles with up to ten warheads, giving each submarine terrifying firepower. New designs are particularly important for China and India, as their current submarines are regarded as too 'noisy' for deployments far from their own shores.

A recently revived concept seeing new discussion for naval nuclear forces is that of 'Third Strike' capability. The term originated during the Cold War as a concept to survive an enemy's first strike designed to devastate military and industrial capacity and a second strike aimed to finish the destruction of whatever remains. The third strike would essentially finish off an enemy and might come months or years later, as the devastated nation starts to rebuild. In this case the point might not be defence so much as simple destruction and vengeance. A ballistic missile submarine which survived a nuclear war up to that point would provide the capability to deliver that third, perhaps final, attack.

LEFT: In this still taken from video, a Russian Bulava sea-launched ballistic missile rises from the sea during testing, following the smoke trail of two previous launches. Russian Navy

BOTTOM: The Type 094 Jin-class serves as China's current ballistic missile submarine until the replacement Type 096 arrives. It carries a dozen nuclear missiles. US Navy

BELOW: Nuclear-tipped anti-submarine weapons like this, launched from a US destroyer in 1962, had been resigned to the history books, but the possibility of nuclear-armed autonomous weapons now looms for the future. US Navy

AUTONOMOUS SHIPS AND SUBMARINES

Robotic vessels of war

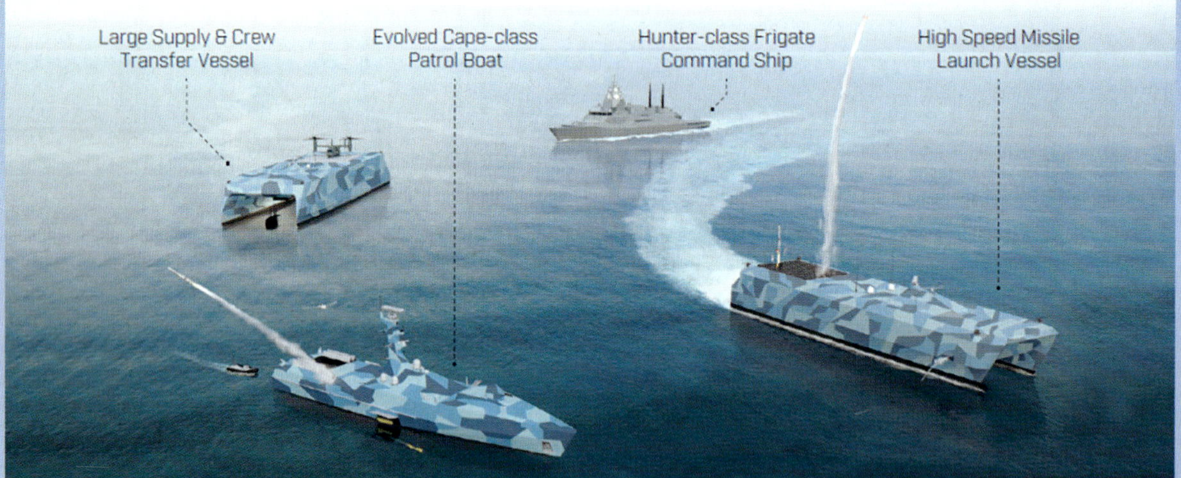

RIGHT: This graphic demonstrates the relationship between a manned command ship and the USVs it can control. Each USV can also deploy their own smaller USVs and UUVs. Austal

As Artificial Intelligence (AI) and robotics technologies advance, the world's navies are creating warships and submarines capable of autonomous operations. These uncrewed vessels have the potential to radically alter the conduct of naval warfare. Numerous prototypes are in development and testing around the world and new designs are rapidly increasingly in size, capabilities and complexity.

Autonomous capability actually denotes two separate mission sets. The first is true autonomy, a vessel able to sail entirely on its own, carry out a mission, and return to port unaided. The second is as part of a squadron or fleet of vessels, some crewed, some uncrewed. Depending on how they are equipped and armed, the autonomous vessels would be controlled by crewed command ships and used for reconnaissance, mine countermeasures, escort or offensive strikes.

There are advantages to Unmanned Surface Vessels (USV) and Unmanned Underwater Vessels (UUV). They don't need extensive berthing and life support facilities for a crew, so the space saved can be allocated for additional fuel, sensors and weapons. They are also useful for dangerous missions, such as minesweeping or reconnaissance in enemy held waters.

Some designs are 'optionally manned' and have minimal facilities for a crew. Autonomous and AI-controlled weapons systems are not yet trusted to control lethal weapons. This allows a crew to be accommodated in case human decision-making is needed or to solve command and control or ethical issues as the technology matures. As with Unmanned Aerial Systems (UAS), armed USVs and UUVs will require commands from a human controller to fire. It will likely take decades of maturation, testing and field use before ethically minded military forces will trust lethal force entirely to an autonomous system. That, or a desperate need during wartime.

USVs have the potential to allow a naval force enormous increases in firepower and flexibility using fewer sailors. They can act as scouts, minesweepers or logistics vessels. The US Marine Corps is investigating the use of UUVs and low-observable USVs as resupply ships for units stationed on islands in contested seas. Using USVs for these auxiliary missions keeps more sailors out of harm's way using hulls which are cheaper and faster to build.

As combat ships are compelled to operate in dispersed groups, armed USVs provide a way to vastly increase firepower and the density of missile salvoes. Currently, battle fleets have a limited number of launch tubes aboard each ship. These launch tubes can carry a mix of anti-aircraft, anti-ship and land attack missiles and commanders must plan carefully to best employ their limited number of weapons. Soon, each cruiser, destroyer or frigate might control several USVs, each with dozens or hundreds of launch tubes, greatly increasing options

BELOW: Two USVs trail the Littoral Combat Ship USS *Gabriele Giffords* during a Pacific exercise. Using the LCS design as a command ship for USVs brings a new capability to this controversial warship design. US Navy

for commanders and enabling a fleet to stay in action longer. Other USVs might be configured for anti-air or anti-submarine warfare. Specialised designs could act as electronic warfare ships or as decoys, projecting a larger electronic signature to draw enemy missiles away from crewed combatants.

USVs are also useful for smaller operations in littoral zones and riverine warfare. A smaller crewed warship such as a frigate, corvette or patrol craft might similarly control its own small squadron. For example, a crewed frigate might sit offshore, deploying a few small patrol craft which can operate in shallower waters and rivers. Several UAS fly overhead, searching for targets or threats. Small robotic UUVs accompany the patrol craft upriver, searching for mines, blockages and their enemy counterparts. An armed USV shadows the frigate, its launch tubes supplying plenty of ordnance for strikes once the enemy is located. A logistics USV keeps the entire force supplied and in action.

The Royal Navy is embracing the possibilities of USVs and UUVs. In March 2025, the service took delivery of the first of the Ariadne class of USVs, optimised for mine warfare. The Royal Navy launched CETUS, a large UUV intended as a technology demonstrator, the same month. The Australian Navy's Ghost Shark large UUV is a modular design undergoing testing. In 2023 Turkey fired a cruise missile from a small USV, proving the concept of a USV as a combatant vessel.

The US Navy is committed to widespread use of autonomous vessels and plans to incorporate dozens of them into its battle fleet. Though it does not yet appear to have armed any of its USVs, the ships of the USN's USV Squadrons (USVRONs), nicknamed the 'Ghost Fleet,' are seeing use in numerous exercises. In late 2023 two USVs were controlled by the Littoral Combat Ship USS *Gabrielle Giffords* during a Pacific Fleet Exercise. The LCS is widely seen as a failed design for a warship but could have a future controlling squadrons of USVs.

ABOVE: This concept image shows a crewed ship controlling its own small fleets of USVs, UUVs and UAS, all in concert with a submarine. Saab

LEFT: The Australian navy's Ghost Shark UUV uses a modular design to carry different packages of sensors, smaller vehicles and eventually weapons. Australian Government

LEFT: The Chinese navy (PLAN) has been testing a trimaran design for several years. Note the rounded features, suggesting experimentation with a stealth design. Chinese MoD

UNMANNED SYSTEMS

Drones for a war at sea

ABOVE: The Turkish Navy has created the world's first drone carrier with the *Anadolu*, which carries a mixed air wing of manned helicopters and multi-mission UAS. US Navy

The use of Unmanned Aerial Systems (UAS) has rapidly expanded in the past three decades. The first UAS served as reconnaissance and surveillance platforms but soon evolved into other roles, including strike, close air support and recently aerial refuelling. The Ukraine War has seen the proliferation of loitering munitions, also known as 'suicide' or 'kamikaze' drones. These are essentially expendable munitions used to attack targets with precision.

Future UAS systems promise to vastly increase the capability of existing and future aircraft carriers. Large carriers can embark a wider variety of aircraft, improving the effectiveness of the air wing. These include refuelling tankers, early warning and Electronic Warfare (EW) models. Using smaller UAS for these roles will provide an airwing room aboard ship for more aircraft and reduce the number of pilots and aircrew who must be risked on combat operations. The US Navy is already testing the MQ-25 Stingray in the tanker role, with the promise of using it in other roles in the future. A UAS squadron aboard a US supercarrier will be a versatile asset.

Smaller carriers or those configured for Vertical/Short Take Off/Landing (V/STOL) operations cannot currently operate such specialised aircraft at all. During the Falklands crisis, for example, the Royal Navy's (RN) carrier task force lacked such early warning, EW and tanker aircraft, making operations more difficult and riskier. The British Queen Elizabeth-class ships also currently lack such platforms, but the RN is developing a series of UAS to fill these roles. Such UAS would dramatically increase the combat power of the carrier without a corresponding increase in crew and logistics requirements.

UAS have also given rise to the drone carrier, an aircraft carrier which carries only unmanned systems. China built the first ship purpose-designed as a drone carrier, *Zhu Hai Yun*, though it reportedly serves as an oceanographic research vessel. Another Chinese drone carrier is believed to be under construction. Other nations have adapted existing ships as drone carriers. Turkey did so with the amphibious assault ship *Anadolu*, with South Korea and Portugal testing the concept as well. The Turkish ship carries improved versions of the Bayraktar drones used successfully in the early months of the Ukraine War. These ships also carry manned helicopters.

Iran built an improvised drone carrier, the *Shahid Bagheri*, by installing flight decks atop the hulls of a former commercial ship (see page 106). The flight deck is angled and leads to a ski-jump style ramp

BELOW: The Proteus UAS promises to fill anti-submarine, cargo and other roles for the Royal Navy. In this image a Proteus is dropping sonobuoys to locate an enemy submarine. Leonardo

ABOVE: An F-35 with its 'squadron' of UAS to support and enhance its capabilities. The pilot will control and deploy the UAS for different missions, using advanced control systems to manage them. Lockheed Martin

RIGHT: The US Navy's MQ-25 Stingray UAS can perform aerial refuelling, surveillance and reconnaissance duties. It has a range of 500 miles with its Rolls-Royce turbofan engine. Boeing

at the bow. This ship also operates manned helicopters and has hatches on its sides to launch small boats via a crane.

UAS also promise to increase the capabilities of manned aircraft. An advanced strike aircraft like the F-35 will be assigned a number of UAS, making each aircraft its own squadron. Each plane might have several armed UAS for strike support, several more for reconnaissance and surveillance and yet more for electronic warfare. Controlling all these UAS while operating the manned aircraft will require the pilot to have assistance from advanced command and control systems.

The naval portion of the Ukraine War (see page 78) has also given rise to 'sea drones,' essentially small expendable boats filled with explosives which can attack ships or port facilities. The Ukrainian Magura series achieved extensive success against Russian naval vessels as part of a complex campaign designed to attrit Russian naval capability. While they can be destroyed with gunfire and their command linkage can be jammed, their use complicates Russian naval planning and operations.

Also known by the nickname 'Sea Baby,' the Ukrainians have expanded them into a multipurpose platform, able to carry .50-cal machine guns, thermobaric grenade launchers and even infrared seeking missiles such as the Sidewinder and Atoll. The Ukrainians have claimed several hits against Russian tactical aircraft, helicopters, and patrol boats with these new versions. Another version is dedicated to intelligence gathering and mine countermeasures.

Ukrainian ingenuity in this new field of unmanned systems portends their widespread use globally, particularly by smaller powers who cannot afford a large fleet. However, in the event of war, such new weapons are likely to be used by everyone involved, as they promise capability, low expense and effectiveness. UAS are similarly bound to further proliferate across the world's navies.

RIGHT: The Lightweight Affordable Novel Combat Aircraft (LANCA) is a concept to provide the Royal Navy with a UAS able to perform strike or aerial refuelling missions at need. UK MoD Crown Copyright

CLIMATE CHANGE

Effect of a warming world on naval operations

While the causes of climate change are controversial to many, the effects of a warmer world may have serious implications for future warfare at sea. Warmer sea waters, more energetic storms, sea level rise and erosion of current coastlines all factor into where and how navies will fight their coming battles. Around the world, military organisations are devising ways to prepare for expected environmental changes and planning for how best to aid their civilian populations from an adversary which cannot be defeated through combat.

There are several ways in which climate changes directly affect military operations, including:

Surface ships: Higher air and water temperatures reduce the efficiency of propulsion and cooling systems aboard ship. This leads to increased fuel consumption, requiring more frequent refuelling, always a logistics concern. Maintenance needs also increase as does the frequency of breakages requiring repair. Warmer air and shipboard temperatures affect the performance of crews just as they do soldiers on land, reducing crew performance and requiring shorter working shifts and increased shift rotations while at sea. Future warships will need more robust air conditioning systems for crew and electronics.

Submarines: Warmer sea waters have different levels of salinity and acidity. These differences can change the way sound propagates underwater. This can change the effectiveness of sonar systems, affecting both the ability of a submarine to hide and how well surface ships can detect them. Marine life grows differently in warmer water; one submariner told the author that submarines operating in warm waters even now must clean out their heat exchangers more regularly than in the past as clams will actually start to grow in them. Apparently, cleaning out the exchangers when this happens is a very smelly and unpleasant task.

Aircraft: Warmer air is less dense, creating less lift for aircraft. To compensate they must use more fuel or carry smaller payloads. This can force aircraft to make more sorties or require more aircraft per strike to deliver the same ordnance on target or to carry supplies. All of this increases maintenance needs. Warmer air also affects cloud cover, presenting challenges to visibility, line of sight and ceiling. All of this must be considered during mission planning and execution.

ABOVE: American and Canadian ice breakers work together in the Arctic Ocean. Warming water means areas with ice sheets currently too thick for ships will become navigable. US Coast Guard

Electromagnetic Systems: Variations in air temperature, clouds, rain, humidity and winds can affect how well radar and communications equipment perform. Lasers, whether used as weapons or for range finding, can be seriously affected by clouds and dust.

Wind and Storms: Warmer water and air can change the speed and direction of winds, which can change surface waves. A warmer atmosphere causes more water evaporation leading to higher humidity and increased rainfall. Hurricanes, typhoons and common storms can be made more intense and longer by such conditions. Winds and storms increase fuel use and repair needs for ships and aircraft. Storms also damage naval bases and ports.

Sea-level rise and melting permafrost are especially dangerous for naval forces as they must operate from coastal bases. Even a small increase in sea levels can lead to

BELOW: A British reconnaissance aircraft observes a newly separated iceberg off the South Sandwich Islands. Icebergs threaten navigation and require monitoring. UK MoD Crown Copyright

larger storm surges during hurricanes and typhoons, for example. Damage to base and port facilities will prevent or slow ship resupply, refuelling and dockyard repairs.

Higher seas also penetrate farther inland, contaminating fresh water used for drinking, which affects the populations navies are dedicated to protecting. Navies already routinely respond to cities hit by major storm surges; sea level rise will increase the frequency of such responses. Many nations and regions are at risk from sea level rise and navies will be expected to operate in these expanded littoral zones. The loss of cities along the coasts will also force populations to migrate, likely to cause conflict as they seek to take land and resources from the existing occupants.

China, for example, has 11,185 miles of coastline and 6,700 islands, all of which are vulnerable to the effects of sea level rise. As with other nations, its largest population centres are along the coasts. As China's coastal regions lose land and potable water, its citizens will need to be relocated. Higher seas mean higher river levels as well, and China already suffers from occasional flooding of its major rivers. This will affect farming output and power generation from the Three Gorges Dam.

Sea level rise will naturally be accompanied by shrinking ice caps at the poles. Many nations are preparing for the new resources and navigable waters which smaller ice caps will reveal, and they are preparing to fight for those resources as well. Russia is building extensive new military facilities along its northern coast and Arctic islands in anticipation of its northern sea route becoming open year-round. As this route runs mostly along their border, it will be easier for them to control. It also considerably shortens the distance shipping must sail from Asia to Europe. For example, the route from Korea to Holland is shortened by 4,000 nautical miles by taking this route. Such a valuable shipping route is bound to attract conflict in a future war.

ABOVE: HMS *Portland* battles high waves during rough weather off the coast of Norway. Storms and wind make normal navigation difficult, combat operations even more so. UK MoD Crown Copyright

LEFT: An RAF Chinook helicopter plugging a breach in the River Steeping, Wainfleet, Lincolnshire in 2019. Climate change threatens coastal and river regions with heavy rainfall and storm surges. UK MoD Crown Copyright

LEFT: UK Royal Marines operate an assault boat during training in Norway. As coastlines change, small boats will be needed to navigate the shallows of newly flooded areas. UK MoD Crown Copyright

THE ARCTIC

A thawing future battleground

RIGHT: A trio of curious polar bears inspect the attack submarine USS *Honolulu*. A conflict in the Arctic would disrupt the ecosystem these animals depend upon. US Navy

For decades during the Cold War, naval forces operating in the Arctic were almost entirely limited to icebreakers, small research missions and nuclear submarines. Ice dominated the region, covering land and sea alike, much of it year-round. The concept of fighting a war in the Arctic centred mostly around submarines fighting duels under the ice cap, though what they would have been fighting over was nebulous at times. Extracting natural resources there proved difficult and rarely profitable.

This situation is changing rapidly, and nations are rushing to be competitive in this new realm. While the world in general is warming, the Arctic is experiencing temperature increases much faster than the rest of the world. Since humans began measuring polar ice using satellites some 46 years ago, the summer Arctic sea ice extent is shrinking by 12.2% per decade, according to NASA. As the icecap decreases, it reveals regions previously inaccessible to exploitation. Some of the world's largest oil and gas deposits are in the Arctic. Thirteen percent of undiscovered oil and 30% of undiscovered natural gas is located above the Arctic Circle. Eighty-five percent of these deposits are offshore with the heaviest concentrations believed to be near Greenland, Alaska, Russia and near the North Pole.

If these predictions are even close to accurate, they point to massive economic wealth and energy sources, providing ample reason for conflict. Nations and groups which border the Arctic are all increasing their military capabilities for operating in the area, including Russia, the United States, Canada, and nations of the European Union. Several states which do not border the Arctic are also tailoring forces to operate there, including the United Kingdom, Japan, China, and France. While there are initiatives to negotiate future exploitation of the region, there is a general acknowledgement that conflict in the Arctic is increasingly likely.

A 2024 US Naval War College (NWC) report gathered information through naval officers and academics from Canada, Denmark, Finland, Iceland, Norway, Sweden, the US, France, Japan, and the UK. While they concluded a direct threat from Russia or China to NATO territory

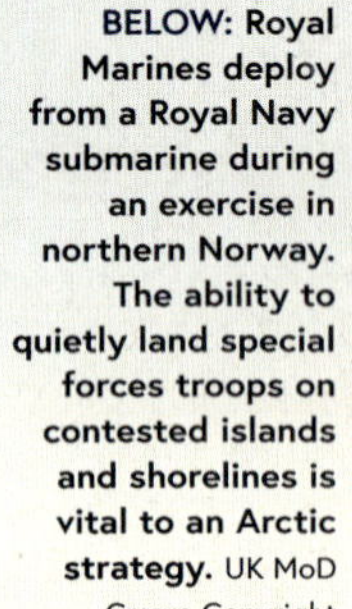

BELOW: Royal Marines deploy from a Royal Navy submarine during an exercise in northern Norway. The ability to quietly land special forces troops on contested islands and shorelines is vital to an Arctic strategy. UK MoD Crown Copyright

ABOVE: Mine warfare is sure to be a part of an Arctic conflict. This is the Russian minesweeper *Vladimir Gumanenko*, assigned to the Northern Fleet. Russian MoD

BELOW: A pair of Skjold-class corvettes of the Royal Norwegian Navy. Manoeuvrable, stealthy and heavily armed, these small ships could easily strike enemy ships from fjords and rivers. UK MoD Crown Copyright

is unlikely in the near term, actions short of war are more likely as nations test the limits of what might be achieved. Actions short of war include sabotage of pipelines, cutting of undersea cables, and jamming of communications with Arctic outposts and facilities. Such activities are hard to attribute, cause confusion and are relatively inexpensive to conduct but expensive in their results for the nations attacked.

The NWC authors did conclude Russia poses a long-term threat to NATO in particular, due to their relative proximity and Russian fears of being encircled, as the Soviet Union was during the Cold War. Russia possesses a long Arctic coastline which will become accessible through more of the year as the ice recedes. It has established extensive ground, air and sea forces in the region earmarked for Arctic warfare. The Russians are also constructing new bases in the Arctic and reopening ones from the Cold War.

China is also preparing forces for service in the Arctic, including a class of icebreakers which could support its nuclear submarine fleet. It also operates research stations in Iceland, and on Svalbard Island, north of Norway. While these are nominally scientific outposts, they are believed to also serve military purposes, such as intelligence gathering.

Chinese-Russian cooperation in the Arctic is seen as a growing threat to Western nations and the NATO alliance. In 2023 a combined force of Russian and Chinese ships sailed near Alaska and the Aleutian Islands, closely monitored by the US Navy. A similar force sailed in the region in 2021.

In response, other powers have begun their own preparations for Arctic operations. Members of NATO with Arctic territory are particularly eager to increase the alliance's capabilities to deter Russian aggression. The NWC report concluded that increased cooperation between the US, NATO, Japan and other aligned nations is required.

The UK takes part in this effort through leadership in the Joint Expeditionary Force (JEF), composed of military assets from northern European countries designed for quick responses to crises. Combining the experience these nations possess in Arctic operations gives the JEF extensive capability in submarine and anti-submarine warfare, amphibious operations and intelligence gathering. In an emergency it could form an international battle group including aircraft carriers such as the Queen Elizabeth-class, icebreakers when needed, and a large number of small combatant vessels operated by all the northern navies.

Less often discussed is the potential for similar conflict in the Antarctic. A treaty governs this region, which has partly kept tensions low. The Antarctic's greater remoteness to major powers and difficulty in extracting resources there also play a role in keeping the area peaceful – for now. However, as the ice there also recedes, land and natural resources will likely be exposed in time, raising the likelihood of conflict there as well.

COAST DEFENCE

Keeping the enemy at a distance

Navies control the seas, but humanity lives on land. Naval operations ultimately occur to support the objectives their country's economic or political goals. Only the navies of large, wealthy nations can afford the ability to support substantial naval forces far from their own shores, known generally as power projection. The vast majority of the world's navies operate in coastal areas, close to home, protecting their own local interests. Most navies are coastal defence forces. These forces can only project power locally, against a neighbouring state or an enemy force operating nearby.

Currently coastal defence is thought of in terms of Anti-Access/Area Denial (A2/AD). This term encompasses a layered effort to keep an enemy from entering a contested zone or geographic area and imposing its will. For naval warfare this means keeping an enemy away from your coastline or a piece of critical terrain, such as the entrance to the Persian Gulf. Examples of successful A2/AD defences in British history include the campaign against the Spanish Armada and the Battle of Britain.

For a coastal defence or A2/AD plan to succeed, it must take advantage of local geography, such as features of the coastline or offshore islands. Constricted terrain or water features are vital as they limit the attacker's options; without such restrictions the attacker will have more options than can be defended against. The English Channel, Taiwan Strait and Strait of Hormuz are all examples.

Once geography is considered, defences must be assembled which can reasonably succeed against attack. Since the defender has the advantage of land-based defences, they can employ multi-domain assets. Land based anti-ship and anti-aircraft missiles, mines, strike and patrol aircraft, armed helicopters and even long-range artillery can be combined against an attack. A realistic A2/AD plan will incorporate land, sea, air, cyber, information and space assets, if the defender has access to them.

Small patrol boats and fast attack craft can be built cheaply in large numbers and sortie from ports, rivers or behind islands or peninsulas. After firing a salvo of missiles, they quickly retire to reload. Helicopters are similarly useful as they can hide behind terrain features and land on unimproved ground, coming out to fire and falling back to prepare for the next mission. Their lower carrying capacity is a disadvantage, but even attack helicopters armed with small anti-tank missiles can be a threat to smaller warships, transports and landing craft.

Electronic Warfare (EW) assets along the coast also make enemy operations more difficult. If that enemy is using GPS-guided weapons, then GPS jammers will reduce their accuracy, forcing an enemy to expend more ordnance and use more sorties of combat aircraft to destroy a given target. Such jammers are limited in their effectiveness, however, as they also emit a signal which can be located and targeted. EW is a two-way street.

A good A2/AD plan mixed with other elements of national policy can achieve the preferred state of deterrence, where no attack occurs because the attacker does not think they can succeed at an acceptable cost. Deterrence is less likely if an opponent has greater numbers, technological overmatch or local allies to provide basing and support. One or more of these factors are important to US plans in the event of war with Iran, North Korea or China. In the Persian Gulf, for example, the US could base land forces in allied territory, providing long range rocket and missile artillery, air defence and EW assets to support naval forces.

Notably, as naval A2/AD defences often centre on restricted water features with shallow depths, this can limit the use of large attack submarines, which may be forced to operate at the periphery or launch long-range attacks with cruise missiles. Small coastal defence or mini-sub designs are more useful.

BELOW: Air defence weapons such as this NASAMs missile system are vital to keep opposing aircraft at a distance. Destroying them and their fire control radars is a painstaking, methodical process for an attacker. Kongsberg Defence

LEFT: A Japanese Ground Self-Defense Force Type 12 anti-ship missile launcher firing. A new version of the missile will have a range of 540 miles. US Army

Reducing coastal defences is a methodical process. An attacker will first focus on the greatest threats; long range missiles, aircraft, air defences and naval vessels. Cyber-attacks will be unleashed against EW and command and control systems. For forces with extensive air power, achieving air supremacy is vital to gaining freedom of action. Destroying an enemy's coastal defences allow the attacker freedom to range that coastline, striking where and when they desire.

How long the operation continues depends on its objectives. The Ukrainians have succeeded in keeping Russian forces from most of their coastline but the war continues as of writing. An objective of destroying an opponent's offensive assets might be accomplished in days or a few weeks. In a major war, it could take much longer. At their start, most conflicts are predicted to end quickly. History has shown that is often not the case. The Japanese created an A2/AD defence across the Western Pacific by mid-1942 during World War Two. It took the Allies three years of painstaking effort to destroy it, but they were ultimately victorious. Another Pacific war against a Chinese defence could easily take as long.

LEFT: Coastal defence incorporates electronic warfare and GPS jamming systems to hinder enemy precision munition accuracy and communications and to geolocate enemy forces by tracking their signals. Russian MoD

BELOW: Smaller navies rely largely on fast attack craft such as this Turkish Ares 55. They can hide in ports, fjords or rivers, pop out to launch missiles, and retire just as quickly. Ares Shipyard

FLEET ACTIONS

Naval warfare on a large scale

ABOVE: Fleet battles in a major war will almost certainly include multinational forces. Here, ships of the United States, Japan, Singapore and South Korea exercise together. US Navy

A primary feature of naval warfare since 1945 has been the distinct lack of large-scale actions between opposing fleets. During that period, the US Navy (USN) held command of the seas and the conduct of the Cold War prevented a real challenger from arising. Compared to World War Two, purely naval actions in the last eight decades have been almost miniscule, involving small numbers of ships which would have rated as only minor actions during that conflict.

As great power competition returns, the chance of a major war increases. China's rise and the concern this causes the West is the major factor in this evolving situation, making a naval war between China, and the US along with its allies the most expected scenario. While the Chinese desire to absorb Taiwan is the most touted issue, China must also guard its trade routes and secure the import of resources needed to keep its economy functioning. In the coming decades China will certainly join other nations in searching for new resources in the oceans, the Arctic and elsewhere, increasing the chance of conflict.

Major powers going to war means fleet actions, larger and more destructive than any naval battles since 1945. In the 21st century, fleets will have to contend with missile salvoes, air attack, submarine attack, UAS, space-based surveillance, cyber-attacks and electronic warfare. Due to this plethora of technological threats, modern navies are experimenting with ways to protect their forces while retaining the ability to mass fire on a target at sea or on shore. Modern warships are

RIGHT: China has focused on creating a navy which can protect its homeland and project power along its sea lines of communication. Here the destroyer *Kaifeng* operates with the fleet supply ship *Hulunhu*. Chinese MoD

RIGHT: Photographs of fleets in formation are visually interesting but in action such a task force would be spread out over many miles of ocean. UK MoD Crown Copyright

complex, expensive and take years to build, meaning no navy can afford to lose too many of them too quickly.

Current thought leans toward forces which are distributed and networked. Distribution means platforms, whether ships, aircraft, submarines or land-based weapons are spread out over distance to reduce their vulnerability. For such forces to coordinate their fire effectively, they must be networked into a solid system of communication. This is required to ensure they can mass sufficient fires against a target so as to overwhelm its defences. If they cannot time their attacks properly, missile and air strikes would come in piecemeal.

For example, assume a USN task force consisting of a Carrier Strike Group (CSG), a Surface Action Group (SAG) of several destroyers and frigates, and a missile-equipped attack submarine are dispersed across several hundred square miles of ocean to avoid detection and engagement. Their mission is to engage an enemy carrier task force. The task force's vertical launch tubes have a mix of air defence, anti-submarine and anti-ship weapons. Once their target is located and its defensive capability assessed, the task force will calculate how much ordnance is needed to overcome it.

The attack will be a mix of aircraft ordnance from the carrier and missiles from the SAG and CSG escorts. The aircraft and missile launches must carefully timed so the ordnance arrives simultaneously. The task force's planning officers will calculate times of flight and speed for each ordnance type, considering the location of each firing unit. Such a strike takes complex planning and careful positioning of ships and aircraft, so they are no closer to the target than needed to range it.

The ships fire Maritime Strike Tomahawk cruise missiles (1,000 miles range), SM-6 missiles in anti-ship mode (150 miles), Naval Strike Missiles (115 miles) and Harpoon missiles (80 miles). The strike aircraft fire Long Range Anti-ship Missiles (LRASM – 350 miles) and may carry air-launched Harpoons. If the submarine takes part, it can launch Tomahawks and Harpoons. Such a strike takes complex planning and careful positioning of ships and aircraft, so they are no closer to the target than needed to range it. The SM-6 is supersonic, while the rest of the anti-ship missiles are subsonic, further illustrating the planning complexities.

The target has an equally complex task in defending from the incoming strike. It will use electronic warfare systems and chaff, radar and infrared decoys designed to draw missiles away from a ship, to confuse some of the incoming weapons. Air defence missiles with interceptor capability are the next line of defence, followed by close-in weapons systems such as cannon and short-range missiles. The defending task force may have only a minute or so to engage any sea-skimming missiles, as they will only be visible at about 15 miles due to the curvature of the earth.

After the strike hits the target, the USN task force will have to assess whether a second strike is needed. It must also move to avoid being attacked itself. Once it has expended enough ordnance, it will also need to retire for reloading and refuelling. Fleet battles will be a complicated matter of reconnaissance, manoeuvre, attack, defence and withdrawal, all happening simultaneously.

BELOW: The Russian Navy has few large surface ships in service and these could not project power far from its coastline in the event of war. Its submarine fleet remains a larger threat. Note the smoke pillars in the background, from ships firing defensive countermeasures. Russian MoD

SEABED WARFARE

Resources and data on the ocean floor

LEFT: *Belgorod* is Russia's most capable submarine for seabed warfare operations. It is capable of espionage, surveillance and offensive operations. Russian MoD

Submarines have long made the waters below the ocean's surface a battleground. Increasingly, that battlefield is spreading deeper, to the ocean floors. It is a realm of darkness, crushing pressure and uneven terrain. This is bad enough in the littoral zones and shallows, and even worse in the deep ocean, where the bottom is beyond the crush depth of a submarine's hull.

Despites the risks and the harsh environment, the seabeds are vital to the future of the global economy. This is partly about natural resources and the conflicts which will occur to secure control of them. Electrical transmission lines along with oil and gas pipelines are also vital, moving energy resources from place to place. The destruction of a pipeline can deny millions of people the fuel for heating, cooking and transportation.

The other major resource on the seabed is digital. Over 1.2million kilometres of telecommunications cables cross the ocean floor, providing internet and data access necessary for the way the 21st century world operates. The US government reports 95% of intercontinental internet traffic moves through undersea cables. Losing even a portion of these cables would seriously curtail not only civilian economic activity but military operations as well.

Most of these resources and networks are in shallow waters and the littorals, putting them within effective range of existing submarines and remotely-piloted vehicles (RPV). As the technology improves, autonomous and unmanned undersea vehicles (UUV) are also coming into wide use. Beyond resources and cables, seabed assets are also useful for espionage, surveillance and salvaging undersea wreckage from sunken ships and downed aircraft.

Attacks have already occurred in recent years. In April 2023, a cable connecting Taiwan with the island of Matsu, which Taiwan occupies and claims, was cut, with Taiwan blaming China. In November 2024, two cables under the Baltic Sea were severed. These cables provided data traffic between Sweden, Finland, Lithuania and Germany. A Chinese merchant ship is suspected of dragging its anchor over the cable, either deliberately or accidentally. In early April 2025, the UK discovered Russian sensors hidden on the seabeds surrounding the British Isles, suspected of being placed there to monitor Royal Navy submarines. Two months earlier the UK Defence Secretary reported a Russian intelligence ship entered the UK's exclusive economic zone to map Britain's underwater infrastructure.

Different navies operate various vessels and systems useful for seabed operations. The Royal Navy's new Astute-class submarines reportedly have seabed operations capacity. RFA *Proteus*, a multi-role ocean surveillance ship, has three large UUVs and a multibeam echosounder, a type of sonar used to map the seabed. Other UUVs

BELOW: Seabed operations require a submarine to have specialised chambers to permit divers to exit the vessel at depth. Saab

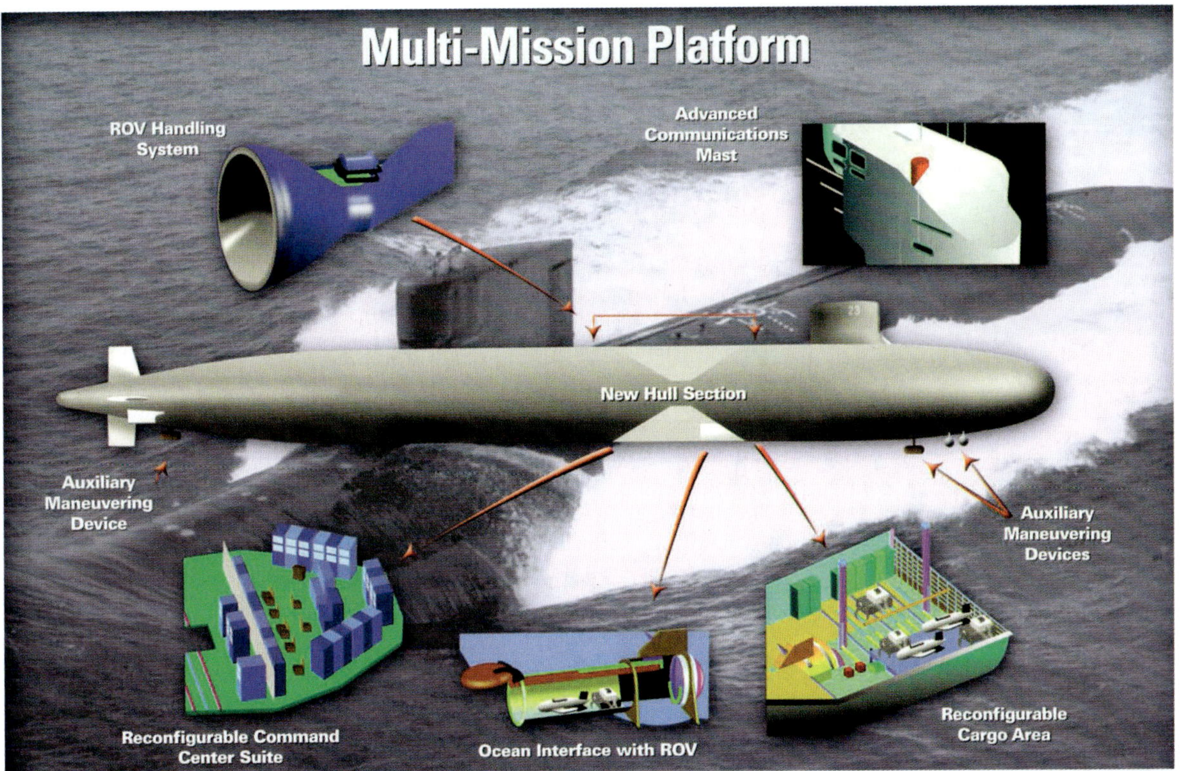

LEFT: USS *Jimmy Carter* received a 100ft extended hull section and other equipment to optimise the submarine for seabed operations. US Navy

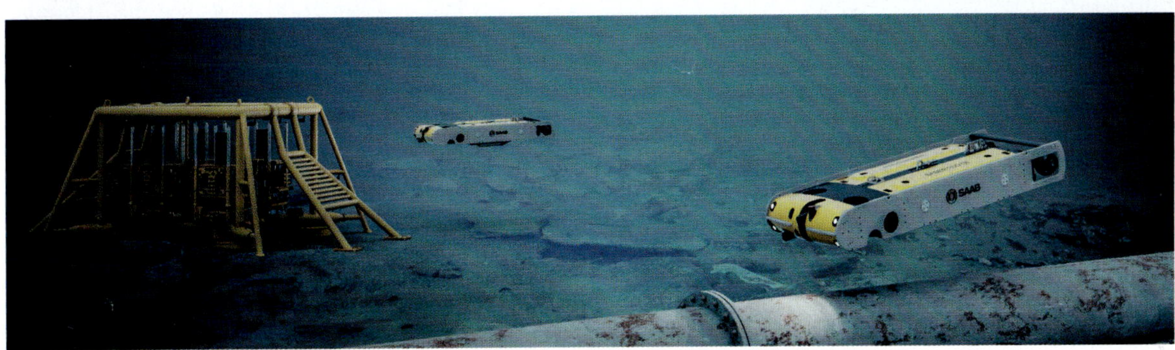

LEFT: Saab's autonomous Sabertooth is an inspection, maintenance and repair system with numerous uses in seabed operations. Saab

are under development and the UK has a partnership with Norway to "counter shared threats in the undersea domain."

France is developing its own seabed warfare capabilities, and considers the seabed as its own warfighting domain, like the land, air or sea. The French Navy added specific departments to its organisation to develop doctrine and tactics and has its own unmanned vehicles which can operate down to 6,000 metres. In March 2025, French naval officials stated intent to extend their capabilities farther from French shores and that offensive capabilities are part of their doctrine.

The United States operates the submarine USS *Jimmy Carter*, a Seawolf-class submarine extensively modified for seabed operations. It is also looking at acquiring an updated version of the Virginia-class attack submarine with seabed capabilities. The US Navy further employs a vast network of undersea sensors and small vehicles (UUVs, RPVs and others).

Russia possesses a substantial fleet of dedicated submarines for seabed operations. Most are small vessels, but two are large submarines. *Belgorod* is a modified Oscar-II cruise missile submarine which can operate UUVs, a nuclear-powered midget submarine and the Poseidon (NATO reporting name *Kanyon*), a nuclear-powered autonomous vehicle. The Poseidon can reportedly be equipped with conventional or nuclear warheads and has unlimited range. The BS-64 *Podmoskovye* is a converted Delta-class ballistic missile submarine which also operates several types of small submarines and UUVs. Both appear to operate as mother ships for Russia's smaller submersibles.

China's seabed warfare assets are little understood through open-source information, though it is certain they are developing new capabilities alongside the other major powers. It does operate a number of research vessels with autonomous systems and unmanned aerial, surface and undersea vehicles. While they are officially not part of the Chinese navy (PLAN), it is known China's civilian fleet oftens works closely with its military.

LEFT: The Leidos Sea Dart is a low-cost UUV which can carry offensive and defensive payloads. It represents a new generation of inexpensive, mass-produced systems for future conflict. Leidos

THE MIDDLE EAST

Hotbed for future conflict

The Middle East has seen a substantial amount of naval activity since 1945, and this will continue in the near future. The region's oil production makes it vital to the global economy and the activities of certain nations and groups continue to draw attention and periodic conflict. The oil-producing states also have the wealth to purchase advanced weapons, and even poorer nations benefit from military aid designed to further the benefactor's goals. This creates client states, further increasing the opportunities for war.

Wars occur regularly across the Middle East, with the latest conflict between Israel, supported by the United States against Iran only the latest chapter. Over the last two decades, the wars in Afghanistan and Iraq, the conflicts between Israel and Hamas, Hezbollah and in Lebanon, and the Libyan Civil War all point to the likelihood of more wars in the future. Syria, its civil war recently ended, will still experience instability as its new government attempts to consolidate and rebuild that shattered nation. Due to the size and vast waterways of the region, naval forces will play major roles in any conflict, even if indirectly.

Iran. Despite its recent defeats, without a major change in governance Iran will continue to be a threat in the region. It struggles against local rivals such as Israel and Saudi Arabia and major powers such as the United States and NATO. The major naval threat posed by Iran is its ability to interdict oil tanker traffic in the Persian Gulf, affecting the world economy and the price of oil. It has also shown the ability to attack the oil production infrastructure of its neighbours, as evidenced by the drone and missile attack on the Saudi oil facilities in September 2019. Iran has also supplied and supported proxy groups in Yemen, Syria and elsewhere.

Iran would interdict traffic in the Gulf much as it did in the 1980s, using mines, small craft and airpower. Shore-based anti-ship missiles and its new drone carrier (see page 92) add to this mix of capabilities. It can attack port facilities and land targets using a wide variety of cruise and ballistic missiles and UAS. Some

ABOVE: The Bahraini fast attack craft *Al Jabiri* trails the destroyer USS *Benfold* during operation in the Middle East. Any combat operation in the Persian Gulf region could quickly involve local forces, which are optimised for the region. US Navy

RIGHT: The navies of the Middle East operate large numbers of smaller warships, such as frigates, corvettes and attack craft. This is the Saudi corvette *Badr*, armed with Harpoon missiles and a 76mm gun. US Navy

RIGHT: A small boat explodes under fire from the destroyer USS *McFaul* during an exercise. Small craft are commonly used by the Iranian Revolutionary Guards Corps for missions in the Persian Gulf. US Navy

RIGHT: The Sa'ar-class corvettes are the largest combatant vessels in the Israeli Navy. They are heavily armed for their size, with large batteries of anti-ship and anti-aircraft missiles. IDF

of its technology is improving due to recent cooperation with Russia following the start of the Ukraine War. Many of its weapons are seeing use in the hands of proxies such as the Houthis, who receive training and assistance from the Iranian Revolutionary Guard Corps (IRGC).

However, Iran's recent defeats at the hands of Israel and the United States show the cracks in the façade of Iranian strength. While the weapons they supplied the Houthis have damaged and even sunk a few merchant ships, they have proven ineffective against Western naval vessels and aircraft. Their air defences are vulnerable to advanced aircraft, as evidenced by the Israeli air strikes in 2024 and 2025 using F-35 stealth fighters and the US attacks by B-2 stealth bombers in June 2025 (as of writing). Naval forces cannot survive without effective air cover and the Iranians lack a credible air force or even air defences. While that has not stopped them from engaging in mining or small boat attacks in the past, it does limit the time they can continue such operations.

While Iran could certainly close the Persian Gulf, how long they could maintain such actions against concerted attack by a coalition naval and air force is questionable. A combination of air and missile strikes on Iran's remaining air defences, along with its coastal, command and control facilities and munitions storage would quickly disorganise Iranian operations. Coalition naval forces would be covered and supported by land and air forces positioned in neighbouring states hostile to Iran. Several of those states have suffered at Iranian hands and would likely want to contribute their own forces to the fighting. Closing the Gulf would also hurt their own shipping.

Israel. At the time of writing, Israel continues its operations in Gaza and elsewhere in response to the Hamas attack of October 7, 2023, though a ceasefire with Iran is in place. Its navy is powerful, capable of defending its coastline and interdicting attempts to supply Hamas via the sea. However, this navy possesses no warships larger than a corvette and is essentially a coastal defence force only able to project power near to its shores. Israel prefers to use air power against more distant threats, and the recent strikes against Iran have shown its effectiveness in air warfare. None of the potential enemies who can directly fight the Israelis have a credible navy, though proxy groups like the Houthis can engage using shore-based missiles and drones.

Whatever future conflicts arise in the Middle East, navies are certain to play an active part. As the region is mostly desert, most of its population lives close to the sea or the few major rivers, making most Middle East nations vulnerable to naval attack. Conversely, they are also within easy reach of naval forces engaged in humanitarian and disaster relief missions as well.

BELOW: Iran has converted several merchant vessels into helicopter/drone carriers, giving them a limited aerial strike capability. This is the *Shahid Bagheri*. Iranian State Media

RUSSIA'S NAVY IN A MAJOR WAR

A mix of capabilities, strengths and weaknesses

If Russia entered into a war with NATO or the United States, its navy would bring a range of strengths and weaknesses into the conflict. Its performance would be largely dependent upon the goals and actions of its opponents. Put bluntly, the Russian Navy has severe limitations both on its ability to project power far beyond its shores and its capability to conduct offensive operations. However, despite its losses and setbacks in the ongoing Ukraine War, the Russian Navy still possesses strengths in key areas useful in a modern war.

The Russian submarine force is by far the most dangerous and capable part of their navy. Russia recognises this and continues to prioritise their submarines, particularly the nuclear-powered vessels. This force includes a dozen ballistic missile submarines which Russia considers vital to its security. There are also two dozen nuclear attack or guided missile submarines, with the rest of the submarine fleet being conventionally powered attack submarines.

The nuclear submarine force would act as Russia's offensive power projection force as they do not require air cover to operate. The conventional submarines would likely remain close to Russia in a primarily defensive role, protecting the coastline and ports. They could also lay mines. Their need to refuel would keep them close to home, as foreign ports would be closed to them. The nuclear submarines could threaten enemy warships, and convoys, with the missile submarines carrying out anti-ship or land attack missions as needed. The Russian Navy is also believed to possess specialty submarines for seabed warfare (see page 104). These could cut internet cables, pipelines and other underwater infrastructure. However, all Russia's submarines would be primary targets of US/NATO anti-submarine forces, which are extensive.

While Russia does operate a number of major surface combatants (cruisers, destroyers and frigates), they would be at extreme risk operating beyond the range of land-based air cover. The sole Russian aircraft carrier, *Kuznetsov*, has been in an extended refit since 2018 and it is uncertain as to whether it will ever return to service. Even if it does, its air wing is small compared to US carriers. If *Kuznetsov* sortied

LEFT: Russian aircraft frequently intercept and harass aircraft from other countries. This SU-35 is flying dangerously close to a USN P-8 Poseidon over the Mediterranean Sea. US Navy

BELOW: In a war with Russia, NATO would quickly form powerful task forces able to contain Russia's surface fleet and protect themselves from Russian nuclear submarines. This NATO task force is led by HMS *Prince of Wales* during Exercise Cold Response 2022. UK MoD Crown Copyright

LEFT: While Russia's surface fleet has limitations, their submarine fleet must be taken seriously. Here HMS *Somerset* escorts a Russian submarine through the English Channel in 2017. UK MoD Crown Copyright

from port, even with a large escort, she would be quickly targeted.

Instead, Russia's major surface combatants could be expected to stay close to home along with Russia's considerable force of small combatants (corvettes, mine warfare and patrol craft). The Russian Air Force, though also somewhat weakened by the Ukraine War, is still quite capable of offensive operations against naval vessels within their range. Together, Russian naval and air forces would form an Anti-Access/Area Denial (A2/AD) force against attacks on Russian territory.

A naval war against NATO could be expected to follow these lines. Russia's nuclear submarines would deploy, perhaps starting a 21st century version of the Battle of the Atlantic, while simultaneously destroying cable and pipelines in the Baltic, Mediterranean and Atlantic. Russian surface combatants in the Black and Baltic Seas would be contained, bottled up in port by superior NATO fleets and geography. The Russian Pacific Fleet at Vladivostok would have trouble deploying as it must sail around Japan, giving the USN opportunities to attack it. The submarine based at Petropavlovsk on the Kamchatka Peninsula would have more freedom of movement, as would the Northern Fleet based at Severomorsk, when not restricted by seasonal ice.

While keeping the Russian Navy on the defensive, conducting offensive naval attacks against Russia would require methodical, slow operations. Russia's radar and air defence network would have to be degraded to allow air superiority or supremacy. For NATO ships to operate near Russia's coast, their air power and shore-based missiles would have to be similarly reduced. This would take time as the Russians have extensive assets to deploy around critical areas and a lot of land in which to hide and move those radars and launchers. Once destroyed or neutralised, air and missile attacks against ships and ports could begin. Attacks in the Black and Baltic Seas would not require extensive naval forces as the closed nature of those waters enable NATO to use land-based assets.

Such a campaign could take months or years; Russia is large, and Russians have proven adept at improvising rough but workable solutions to their shortcomings. The result would likely be NATO naval forces able to operate around the Russian periphery in support of land operations with strikes and perhaps limited amphibious operations.

All of this assumes a conventional war without the use of nuclear weapons. Russia has long stated it would use nuclear weapons to defend its homeland and some consider this a tacit admission that they know their navy could not stand up to NATO or the US. However, Russia has always been a continental power and in the end their navy is not vital to their survival beyond their ballistic missile submarines.

BELOW: A line of Russian warships rehearsing for their Navy Day celebration. Note the large launch tubes for anti-ship missiles. Russian MoD

TAIWAN

The war everyone fears is coming

ABOVE: USS *Carl Vinson* sails with a multinational task force during an exercise in 2024. In a war over Taiwan, US carrier strike groups will be threatened by Chinese long range anti-ship ballistic missiles. US Navy

Analysts and pundits have been predicting a communist Chinese invasion of Taiwan for decades. Officially called the Republic of China (we use Taiwan here for simplicity), the island effectively functions as an independent nation, though it has never declared independence and the People's Republic of China (PRC) has stated such a move would be a red line which would trigger a response. The PRC considers Taiwan essentially a province in revolt and considers reunification an important, non-negotiable goal.

This has led to a delicate and ambiguous political and diplomatic situation concerning the island. The United States does not have a treaty promising to defend or come to Taiwan's aid in the event of a PRC attack but has agreed to maintain the ability to do so and to supply Taiwan with defensive weapons. This is partly to prevent any US President from making promises or taking actions without the consent of the US Congress, but also to maintain a delicate balance between the two entities.

War is far from certain; there are other ways for the situation to be resolved. In the last several years different estimates have been discussed about the timeline for a PRC invasion. Some state it will come in the next few years, by 2028, when the PRC is fully capable of doing so. Another estimate says 2027, the 100th anniversary of the People's Liberation Army. Others say 2030, after the US has reduced its reliance on Taiwan for semiconductors. One theory places an end date for an invasion at about 10-20 years before the centennial of the PRC in 2049, as China will want to give the rest of the world time to 'get over' a Chinese invasion before its centennial celebrations.

If an invasion occurs, it will be preceded by a massive missile and air attack on Taiwan, alongside special forces operations on the island to eliminate leadership and cyberattacks to slow Taiwanese reactions. Chinese naval and air forces will have to quickly get an invasion force across the Taiwan Strait while under fire from whatever Taiwanese forces remain combat capable after the first strike. Just as China has created an Anti-Access/Area Denial (A2/AD) defence to keep the USN away from the Chinese mainland, so too has Taiwan created a A2/AD strategy to defeat or slow a Chinese invasion.

RIGHT: Chinese People's Liberation Army Navy (PLAN) amphibious assault vehicles come ashore during an exercise. In a combat landing on Taiwan these vehicles would face mines, fire from shore, drones and even anti-tank missiles. China MoD

ABOVE: Multi-role frigates like the PLAN *Yueyang* would be vital in escorting a landing force across the Taiwan Strait. It can defend against enemy ships, submarines and missile attack. US Navy

RIGHT: The Taiwanese Navy has invested heavily in small, stealthy, heavily armed attack craft like the corvette *Ta Chiang*, which is designed to operate in the rough seas often seen in the region. ROCN

Taiwan has strived to create a multi-domain defence combining shore-based missiles, naval vessels with missile and torpedoes, air power and layered air defences. Taiwan's geography limits the landing locations for an invader; most of the useful landing sites are at the island's north and west sides. The east side of Taiwan is more mountainous and less conducive to a successful amphibious assault. Taiwan has extensively studied these sites and spent years planning how to best defend them. Weather and sea conditions must also be considered. Researcher Ian Easton has estimated the months of April and October are likely the only times China could move enough troops across the strait to succeed. Once troops are ashore, they must be supplied. Invading Taiwan is not a simple task and could well be the most difficult amphibious assault in history.

If the US does intervene on Taiwan's side, its chances of success depend heavily on how much advance warning it has. The USN would need time to muster its naval and air forces to come to Taiwan's defence. If there is enough time, the US could place ground troops on Taiwan as a tripwire force to prevent a PRC attack in the first place. If such a move fails to deter an attack, those ground forces would be difficult or impossible to supply or reinforce until Chinese naval and air power had been reduced.

China has dedicated extensive effort to creating an A2/AD network of ships, submarines, missiles and aircraft to keep the USN outside the First and Second Island Chains so Taiwan can be isolated during an invasion. Attacks on US bases on Guam, Japan and South Korea could further hamper American plans, though this could bring those nations and their powerful militaries into the conflict. While many think an invasion of Taiwan would be settled in a few weeks at most, once such a war starts, it could stretch into months or years, particularly if there are heavy casualties or the Americans think they were victims of a surprise attack, such as at Pearl Harbor in 1941.

Another scenario is that China does not invade Taiwan but seeks its capitulation through blockade. It could do this through ships and aircraft or through the creation of missile engagement zones set up around the island using land-based missiles. As the USN has proven adept at missile interception, a US response might be the creation of a missile defence 'tunnel' designed to pierce that missile blockade, allowing ships and cargo to reach one of Taiwan's few eastern ports. Such a plan would carry risks for escalation, especially for two nuclear-armed powers.

A RENEWED KOREAN WAR

Conflict around the Korean Peninsula

A renewed conflict on the Korean Peninsula carries a mix of well-understood naval requirements, most of them used in the Korean War of 1950-53, with new factors that have arisen since then. Rationally, a war would be a disaster for North Korea as overall it is badly outmatched in any but the briefest of combats. The North Korean regime's primary goal is its own survival, and wars are unpredictable in both duration and outcome. While the country's leadership often makes aggressive announcements and can appear unstable, it actually acts rationally in its own way and seems to have a sense of when to reduce tensions. However, wars are not always started deliberately; mistake or miscalculation could easily lead to a new war.

North Korea's navy is best described as a coastal defence force, though a large one in terms of total numbers. It can also be thought of as the naval components of North Korea's Anti-Access/Area Denial (A2/AD) force. It operates almost 100 submarines, most of them small coastal models often used to transport special forces troops. Its large surface combatants include a destroyer launched in April 2025 (a sister ship capsized on launching in May 2025 in a well-publicised incident), supported by about 10 frigates and corvettes.

More than 100 missile and torpedo boats are backed up by an equally large number of patrol boats. There are also large numbers of small boats, landing craft and hovercraft, many able to carry troops for landing operations. As North Korea sits at the northern end of the peninsula, its navy is divided into an east and west fleet. These vessels would be supported by the North Korean Air Force along with shore-based missiles and artillery.

South Korea possesses a true blue-water navy, able to deploys ships and small task forces with logistics support away from Korean shores. Many of its 21 submarines can launch anti-ship or cruise missiles and its 30 destroyers and frigates are capable of ocean or coastal operations. These are backed up by a significant force of corvettes and patrol ships, the bulk of them missile-armed. Significantly, the South Korean Navy operates ten large amphibious landing ships, including two amphibious assault ships with flight decks which could be adapted to operate the F-35B fighter. It also has anti-submarine helicopters and patrol aircraft including the P-8 Poseidon and Westland Wildcat.

In the event of war, the South Korean Navy would operate alongside the USN and any other allied navies committed to the conflict. South Korea operates three numbered fleets (1st – 3rd), each with responsibility for a section of the coast to defend. First Fleet protects the east coast and Second Fleet the west, with Third Fleet guarding the south. These fleets would have to extend to cover the North Korean coastline while guarding against North Korean attempts to land special forces and other troops using submarines and small craft. Fast engagements between allied naval vessels and North Korean ships, submarines and coastal defences would be common until attrition becomes too great.

A sustained air campaign using US Carrier Strike Groups and land-based aviation based in South Korea, Guam and possibly Japan to reduce North Korean air defences and shore-based missiles could take weeks or months depending on North Korean skill at hiding and moving their assets. The eventual end result would be a destroyed North Korean air force and a navy sunk or bottled up in port. Mines would be a major weapon as well, just as in the first Korean War. Minesweeping ships and helicopters would be busy and need protection by combatant ships.

US and South Korean amphibious capability could be used to land troops along the coast to outflank or trap North Korean ground forces. However, the good landing points are well-known and would be defended. Naval fire support for allied ground forces could prove a critical

BELOW: Mine Countermeasures (MCM) will play a major role to contain North Korea and prevent damage to allied ships. These are two USN Avenger-class MCMs, the USS *Patriot* and USS *Pioneer.* US Navy

LEFT: A North Korean Amnok-class corvette fires a missile during a demonstration. Analysts believe the ship was built on the hull of a Krivak-class frigate which North Korea received as scrap in the early 2000s. Korean Central News Agency

BOTTOM: American and South Korean ships exercising together. The powerful South Korean Navy, paired with the USN's 7th Fleet, would be a tough opponent for North Korea's aged fleet and limited capabilities. ROK Navy

BELOW: South Korea has a well-developed arms industry able to produce naval vessels. This indigenously built patrol craft is firing a South Korean anti-ship missile. ROK Navy

advantage, particularly as long range missiles could cover the breadth of the peninsula. While the war would still be decided ashore, naval forces would provide needed firepower that North Korea would have trouble countering.

Two new factors add uncertainty to the situation. First, North Korea's nuclear weapons act as a deterrent to a regime-ending campaign. As stated, the regime's goal is survival, and any operation which seemed aimed at toppling it would force a decision from North Korean leadership whether to employ them. Second, unlike in 1950-53, China now possesses significant naval and air forces and has no desire to see extensive US Navy forces operating so close to its coast. While it most likely would exert influence to prevent a war from starting, it could decide to act on its own to resolve a war before the US military arrives in force. China could occupy North Korea itself to maintain the buffer North Korea creates between China and South Korea. It could also offer to give the North to South Korea, allowing the country to reunify – on the condition US forces, nominally no longer needed, leave.

GLOSSARY

The dictionary of naval conflict

ABOVE: The attack submarine USS *Annapolis* surfaced in the Arctic. The region has long been the realm of the nuclear submarine. US Navy

List of Acronyms and Terms

A2/AD	Anti-Access/Area Denial, a system designed to prevent an enemy entering an area you seek to defend
ASROC	Anti-submarine Rocket, a torpedo attached to a rocket motor to extend its range
CAP	Combat Air Patrol, a force of fighters which fly cover over an aircraft carrier or task force to protect it from air attack
CSG	Carrier Strike Group, term for a task force centred around an aircraft carrier
EW	Electronic Warfare
IRGC	Iran Revolutionary Guard Corps, a paramilitary branch separate from the regular Iranian military
LST	Landing Ship, Tank; a type of amphibious warfare ship designed to land armoured vehicles
NATO	North Atlantic Treaty Organisation
PLAN	People's Liberation Army Navy, the Chinese navy
PRC	People's Republic of China, also called communist China or simply China
RAF	Royal Air Force
RN	Royal Navy
ROC	Republic of China, generally known as Taiwan
SAG	Surface Action Group, a USN term for a grouping of surface warships without a carrier
SAM	Surface to Air Missile
SAR	Search and Rescue, usually helicopters assigned to rescue downed pilots or sailors of sunken ships
STUFT	Ships Taken Up From Trade, a UK reserve of cargo and supply ships used in military emergencies
UAS	Unmanned Aerial System
UN	United Nations
UNREP	Underway Replenishment, resupplying a ship at sea
USMC	United States Marine Corps
USN	United States Navy
USV	Unmanned Surface Vehicle
UUV	Unmanned Underwater Vehicle
V/STOL	Vertical/Short Take-Off and Landing

Image credits: Ares Shipyard , Argentine Government, Arun Prakash, Austal, Australian Government, Boeing, Chinese Ministry of Defence, Clandestine Immigration and Naval Museum, Dutch Ministry of Defence, French Navy, General Dynamics, Houthi Movement News, Imperial War Museum, Indian Government, Indian Navy, Iranian State Media , IDF (Israeli Defence Force), Japanese Government, Ken Griffiths, Kongsberg Defence, Korean Central News Agency , Leidos, Leonardo, Lockheed Martin, NARA (US National Archives and Records Administration), Pakistani Air Force, Polish Archives, RAF Historical Branch, ROCN (Republic of China Navy), Republic of Korea Navy, Royal Museums Greenwich, Russian Archives, Russian Ministry of Defence, Russian Navy, SAAB, Toronto Star Archives, UK Ministry of Defence, Ukrainian Ministry of Defence, US Air Force, US Army, US Coast Guard, US Department of Defense, US Marine Corps, US Navy, Yellow Apex